Parley P. Pratt

## A Voice of Warning and Instruction to All People

Or, an introduction to the faith and doctrine of the Church of Jesus Christ

of Latter-day Saints

Parley P. Pratt

**A Voice of Warning and Instruction to All People**
*Or, an introduction to the faith and doctrine of the Church of Jesus Christ of Latter-day Saints*

ISBN/EAN: 9783337175283

Printed in Europe, USA, Canada, Australia, Japan

Cover: Foto ©Lupo / pixelio.de

More available books at **www.hansebooks.com**

# A VOICE OF WARNING

AND

## Instruction to All People;

OR AN

INTRODUCTION TO THE FAITH AND DOCTRINE

OF THE

## CHURCH OF JESUS CHRIST OF LATTER DAY SAINTS.

BY PARLEY P. PRATT.

[REVISED.]

ALSO, AN ANALYSIS OF ISAIAH 29.

---

'BEHOLD, THE FORMER THINGS ARE COME TO PASS, AND NEW THINGS DO I DECLARE; BEFORE THEY SPRING FORTH I TELL YOU OF THEM."—*Isa.* 42:9.

"PRODUCE YOUR CAUSE, SAITH THE LORD; BRING FORTH YOUR STRONG REASONS, SAITH THE KING OF JACOB."—*Isa.* 41:21.

PLANO, ILL.,
PRINTED BY THE BOARD OF PUBLICATION OF THE REORGANIZED CHURCH OF CHRIST.
1877.

# PREFACE

TO THE

## FIFTH REVISED EDITION.

We present this as the Fifth Edition, by the Reorganized Church, of this well known and widely circulated work. Its continued republication is because it has proved to be one of the best means for giving instruction upon the dealings of God with the nations, and upon the gospel of Jesus Christ, that has ever been published, perhaps the best, considering its size and cheapness.

It is in constant demand, being like a small library in itself, in its condensed and yet clear and distinct interpretations of the prophecies and teachings of the Prophets and Patriarchs, of Christ and the Apostles.

In this respect it satisfies the want felt for a more literal rendering of the words of inspired men in their prophetic declarations and teachings; and therein it is an aid to faith in God and to belief in the Scriptures.

In its present form it has the advantage of being in a size that can be bound both in paper and in cloth, the latter being much more preferable for its durability for such constant service; also it is more of a pocket size and not as liable to be broken.

PLANO, Illinois, Nov. 20th, 1876.

# PREFACE

## TO THE FIRST AMERICAN EDITION.

―――・―――

During the last nine years the public mind has been constantly agitated, through all parts of our country, with the cry of "Mormonism, Delusion, Imposture, Fanaticism," &c., chiefly through the instrumentality of the press. Many of the newspapers of the day have been constantly teeming with misrepresentations and slanders of the foulest kind, in order to destroy the influence and character of an innocent society in its very infancy; a society of whose real principles many of them know nothing at all. Every species of wickedness has been resorted to, and all manner of evil has been spoken against them falsely; insomuch, that in many places, houses and ears are closed against them, without the possibility of being heard for a moment. Were this the only evil, we might have less cause of complaint; but in consequence of this, we have been assaulted by mobs, some of our houses have been torn down or burned, our goods destroyed, and fields of grain laid waste. Yea, more, some of us have been stoned, whipped, and shot; our blood has been caused to flow, and still smokes to heaven, because of our religious principles in this our native land, the boasted land of liberty and equal laws, while we have sought in vain for redress, while officers of State have been deaf to the voice of innocence, imploring at their feet for justice, and protection in the enjoyment of their rights as American citizens.

Under these circumstances what could be done? How were we to correct the public mind? We were few in number, and our means of giving information very limited; the columns of most of the papers were closed against us, their popularity being at stake the moment our principles were admitted. It is true we publish a monthly paper, in which our principles are clearly set forth; but its circulation is limited to a few thousands. Under these circumstances, had we the tongue of angels, and the zeal of apostles, with our hearts expanded wide as eternity, with the intelligence of heaven, and the love of God burning in our bosoms, and commissioned to bear as joyful tidings as ever was borne by Michael the Archangel from the regions of glory; yet it would have been as impossible for us to have conmunicated the same to the public, as it was for Paul when he stood in the midst of Ephesus, to declare the glad tidings of a crucified and risen Redeemer; when his voice was lost amid the universal cry, of "great is Diana of the Ephesians." Go lift your voice to the tumultuous waves of the ocean, or try to reason amid the roar of cannon while the tumult of war is gathering thick around, or speak to the howling tempest while it pours a deluge over the plains; let your voice be heard amid the roar of chariots, rushing suddenly over the pavements; or what is still more foolish, converse with a man who is lost in slumber, or reason with a drunkard while he reels to and fro under the influence of the intoxicating poison, and these acts will convince you of the impossibility of communicating truth to that soul who is willing to make up his judgment upon popular rumor; or to be wafted gently down the current of public opinion, without stopping for a moment to listen, to weigh, to hear both sides of the question, and judge for himself. One of the greatest obstacles in the way of the spread of truth in every age, is the tide of public opinion. Let one ray of light burst upon the world in any age, and it is sure to come in contact with the traditions and long established usages of men, and their opinions; or with some religious craft, so that like the Ephesians they counsel together, what shall be done; their great goddess will be spoken against, her magnificence despised, her temple deserted: or what is still worse, their craft is in danger, for by this they have their wealth. Call to mind the apostles in contact with the Jewish Rabbies, or with Gentile superstitions; in short, at war with every religious establishment on the earth. Witness the popular clamor; "If we let them thus alone, all men will believe on them, and the Romans will come and take away our place and nation." "These men that turn the world upside down have come hither also." "What new doctrine is this, for thou bringest certain strange things to our ears?" "These men do exceedingly trouble our city, and teach customs which are not lawful for us to receive and observe, being Romans." "What will this babbler say, he seems to be a setter forth of strange gods?" and many other such like sayings.

Or, let us for a moment contemplate the events of a later date: for instance, the Mother Church against the reformers of various ages; see them belied, slandered, degraded, whipped, stoned, imprisoned, burned, and destroyed in various ways; while the ignorant multitude were made to believe they were the very worst of men. Again, think for a moment of the struggles of Columbus; an obscure individual, of limited education but blessed with a largeness of heart, a noble genius, a mind which disdained to confine itself to the old beaten track. Accustomed to think for himself, he burst the chains which, in ages past, had held in bondage the nations of the earth. He soared aloft, as it were on eagle's wings; outstripped and left far behind the boasted genius of Greece and Rome; penetrated the dark mysteries which lay concealed amid the western waters. Behold him struggling for eight years against the learned ignorance of the courts and councils of Europe; while the sneer of contempt, the finger of scorn, and the hiss of derision, were the solid arguments opposed to his theory. But what was the result when, after many a fruitless struggle, an expedition was fitted out, consisting of three small vessels? A new world presents itself to the wondering nations of the East, destined at no distant period, to become the theatre of the most glorious and astonishing events of the last days. This fact was no sooner demonstrated, than their philosophical, geographical, and religious objections vanished in a moment; haughty ignorance and bigotry were for once constrained to cast their honors in the dust; and bow their reverend heads at the feet of real worth; and learn in humble silence that one fact clearly demonstrated is worth ten thousand theories and opinions of men.

Having said so much to impress upon the human mind the necessity of hearing, and then judging, I would only add, that the object of this publication is to give the public correct information concerning a religious system, which has penetrated every State from Maine to Missouri, as well as the Canadas, in the short space of nine years; organizing churches and conferences in every region, and gathering in its progress from fifty to an hundred thousand disciples; having, at the same time, to sustain the shock of an overwhelming religious influence, opposed to it by the combined powers of every sect in America.—What but the arm of Omnipotence could have moved it forward amid the rage of mobs? Having to contend with the prejudice of the ignorant and the pen of the learned; at war with every creed and craft in christendom; while the combined powers of earth and hell were hurling a storm of persecution, unparalleled in the history of our country.

This work is also intended as a warning voice, or proclamation of truth, to all people into whose hands it may fall, that they may understand and be prepared for the great day of the Lord. Opinion and guess work in the things of God are worse than useless; facts well demonstrated can alone be of service to mankind; and as the Holy Ghost can alone guide us into all truth, we pray God the Eternal Father, in the name of Jesus Christ his Son, that the Spirit of truth may inspire our heart in inditing this matter; that we may be able to write the truth in demonstration of the Spirit and of power; that it may be the word of God, the everlasting gospel, the power of God unto salvation, to the Gentile first, and also to the Jew.

THE AUTHOR.

Nauvoo, 1839.

# Voice of Warning.

## CHAPTER I.

### ON PROPHECY ALREADY FULFILLED.

"We have also a more sure word of prophecy; whereunto ye do well to take heed, as unto a light that shineth in a dark place, until the day dawn and the day star arise in your hearts; knowing this first, that no prophecy of the scripture is of any private interpretation. For the prophecy came not in old time by the will of man; but holy men of God spake as they were moved by the Holy Ghost." (*a*).

In order to prove any thing from Scripture it is necessary to lay down some certain rule of interpretation, without which, the mind is in uncertainty and doubt, ever learning, and never able to come to the knowledge of the truth.

The neglect of such a rule, has thrown mankind into confusion and uncertainty, in all their Biblical researches. Indeed, while mankind are left at liberty to transform, spiritualize, or give any uncertain or private interpretation to the word of God, all is uncertainty.

"Whatsoever things were written aforetime, were written for our learning, that we through patience and comfort of the scriptures might have hope." (*b*).

Now suppose a friend from a distance should write us a letter, making certain promises to us on certain conditions, which if we obtained, would be greatly to our profit and advantage; of course it might be said the letter was written for our profit and learning, that through patience and comfort of the letter we might have hope to obtain the things promised. If we clearly understood the letter, and knew what to expect, it would afford us comfort and hope; whereas, if there was any doubt or uncertainty on our minds in the understanding of the same, we could derive no comfort or hope from the things written, not knowing what to hope for; consequently the letter would not profit us; and so it is with the Scriptures. No

(*a*) 2 Peter 1:19-21.   (*b*) Romans 15:4.

prophecy or promise will profit the reader, or produce patience, comfort, or hope in his mind, until clearly understood, that he may know precisely what to hope for. Now many of predictions of the prophets can be as clearly understood as the almanac when it foretells an eclipse; or else the Bible of all books is of most doubtful usefulness. Far better would it have been for mankind, if the great Author of our existence had revealed nothing to his fallen creatures, than to have revealed a book which would leave them in doubt and uncertainty, to contend with one another from age to age, respecting the meaning of its contents. That such uncertainty and contention have existed for ages, none will deny. The wise and learned have differed, and do still widely differ from each other, in the understanding of prophecy. Whence then this difference? Either revelation itself is deficient, or else the fault is in mankind. To say that revelation is deficient, would be to charge God foolishly; God forbid, the fault must be in man. There are two great causes for this blindness:—

Firstly, mankind have supposed that direct inspiration by the Holy Ghost was not intended for all ages of the Church, but that it was confined to primitive times; that "the canon of Scripture is full;" that all necessary things have been revealed, and that the Spirit which guides into all truth is no longer needed; therefore they sought to understand, by their own wisdom, and by their own learning, what could never be clearly understood, except by the Spirit of truth: for the things of God knoweth no man, except by the Spirit of God.

Secondly, having lost the Spirit of inspiration they began to institute their own opinions, traditions, and commandments; giving constructions, and private interpretations to the written word, instead of believing the things written. And the moment they departed from its literal meaning, one man's opinion or interpretation, was just as good as another's, all were clothed with equal authority, and from thence arose all the darkness and misunderstanding on these points, which have agitated the world for the last seventeen hundred years.

Among the variety of objects which attract the attention of mankind, there is one thing of more value than all others; a principle, which, if once possessed, greatly assists in obtaining all other things worth possessing, whether it be power, wealth, riches, honors, thrones, or dominions. Comparatively few have possessed it, although within the reach of many others, but they were either not aware of it, or did not know its value.

It has worked wonders for those who have possessed it. It enabled some to escape from drowning, while every soul who did not possess it was lost in the mighty deep. It saved others from famine, while thousands perished all around them. By it, men have often been raised to dignity in the State; yea, more, some have been raised to the thrones of empires. The possession of it has sometimes raised men from dungeons to palaces; and there are instances in which those that possessed it were delivered from the flames, while cities were consumed, and every soul, themselves excepted, perished. Frequently when a famine, or the sword, has destroyed a city or nation, they alone who possessed it escaped unhurt. By this time, the reader inquires, What can this thing be? Inform me, and I will purchase it, even at the sacrifice of all I possess on earth. Well, kind reader, this treasure is *foreknowledge*—a knowledge of things future. Let a book be published, entitled, Knowledge of the Future, and let mankind be really convinced that it did give a definite knowledge of future events; so that its pages unfolded the future history of the nations, and of many great events, as the history of Greece or Rome unfolds the past, a large edition would immediately sell at a great sum per copy; indeed it would be above all price. Now, kind reader, the books of the prophets and the Spirit of prophecy were intended for this very purpose. Well did the Apostle say:—"Desire spiritual gifts, but rather that ye may prophesy." (*c*).

Let us enter into the expanded field which lies before us, and search for the treasures of wisdom and knowledge, which have been shining for ages, like a light in a dark place. We will explore regions unknown to many; we will gaze upon the opening glories which present themselves on every side: and feast our souls with knowledge which is calculated in its nature to enlarge the heart, to exalt the mind, and to raise the affections above the little, mean, grovelling things of the world, and make one wise unto salvation.

First, let us understand the rule of interpretation. For this we will not depend on any man, or commentary, for the Holy Ghost has given it by the mouth of Peter, who said:—

"We have also a more sure word of prophecy; whereunto ye do well that ye take heed, as unto a light that shineth in a dark place, until the day dawn and the day star arise in your hearts: knowing this first, that no prophecy of the scripture is of any private interpretation." (*d*).

There is one grand division to be kept in view in the study of prophecy; namely, the distinction between the past and the

(c) 1 Cor. 14:1. (d) 2 Peter 1:19, 20.

future. The reader should be careful to ascertain what portion has been fulfilled, and what remains to be fulfilled; always remembering that Peter's rule of interpretation will apply to both. If we should find in our researches that every prophecy which has been fulfilled to this present year has been *literally* fulfilled, it follows, of necessity, that every prophecy which is yet future, will not fail of a *literal* fulfillment. Let us commence with the days of Noah:

"And behold, I, even I, do bring a flood of waters upon the earth, to destroy all flesh, wherein is the breath of life, from under heaven: and every thing that is in the earth shall die." (*e*).

In the verses which follows the above, the Lord commands Noah to enter the ark and take with him animals of every kind, etc. In the twenty-second verse it is written:—"Thus did Noah, according to all that God commanded him, so did he." (*f*).

It was well for Noah that he was not well versed in the spiritualizing systems of modern divinity; for under their benighted influence, he would never have believed that so marvelous a prophecy would have had a literal meaning and fulfillment. No, he would have been told that the flood meant a spiritual flood, and the ark a spiritual ark, and the moment he thought otherwise, he would have been set down as a fanatic, knave, or fool; but it was so, that he believed the prophecy literally. Here then is a fair sample of foreknowledge; for all the world who did not possess it perished by the flood. The next prediction that we notice is,

"And he [God] said unto Abram, Know of a surety that thy seed shall be a stranger in a land that is not theirs, and shall serve them; and they shall afflict them four hundred years; and also that nation whom they shall serve, will I judge: and afterward shall they come out with great substance. And thou shalt go to thy fathers in peace; and shall be buried in a good old age. But in the fourth generation they shall come hither again: for the iniquity of the Amorites is not yet full." (*g*).

The evil entreating of the children of Israel, four hundred years, together with their coming out with great substance, and the judgments of God upon Egypt, as well as the death of Abraham in a good old age, are all facts too well known to need comment here; suffice it to say, that it is a striking example of the exact fulfillment of prophecy, uttered more than four hundred years before it had its accomplishment. From this we gather that none of those ancient men knew anything of the modern system of spiritualizing. We quote as follows:—

"And the men said unto Lot, Hast thou here any besides? Son-in-law

(*e*) Gen. 6:17. (*f*) Gen. 6:22. (*g*) Gen. 15:13-16.

and thy sons, and thy daughters, and whatsoever thou hast in the city, bring them out of this place ; for we will destroy this place, because the cry of them is waxen great before the face of the Lord ; and the Lord hath sent us to destroy it." (*h*)

Now Lot believed the thing in its literal sense, and took as many of his family as would go with him, and escaped for his life, to the great amusement, no doubt, of the Sodomites, who probably stood gazing after him, crying delusion, delusion; they thinking all the while that the prophecy was only a figure. Here is an example of a man escaping from the flames by foreknowledge imparted to him, while the whole city perished. O what a blessing that Lot had no knowledge of the modern manner of interpreting prophecy! If it had once entered his heart that he must come out of Sodom spiritually, instead of literally, it would have cost him his life.

Let us examine a prophecy of Joseph in the land of Egypt:—

"Behold, there come seven years of great plenty throughout all the land of Egypt : and there shall arise after them seven years of famine ; and all the plenty shall be forgotten in the land of Egypt; and the famine shall consume the land ; and the plenty shall not be known in the land by reason of that famine following : for it shall be very grievous." (*i*)

Joseph then gave directions for corn to be laid up in great abundance during the seven plenteous years, in order to provide against famine. And Pharaoh, being no better versed in the school of modern divinity than his predecessors, never once thought of any other interpretation than the most literal; and thus he was the means, together with Joseph, in the hand of God, in saving, not only their nation, but the house of Israel from famine. This is another striking example of the power of foreknowledge. It not only saved from famine, but it exalted Joseph from a dungeon to a palace; from the lowest degradation to the highest honor; so that they cried before him, "Bow the knee." But oh, what mourning and death would have followed, had they dreamed only of spiritual famine and spiritual corn.

Having given a few examples of early ages, we will present some of the most remarkable instances of prophecy, and its fulfillment, until we come down to the Jewish prophets, where the field opens wide in reference to the most remarkable events of various ages, and terminating in a full development of the opening glories of the last days.

In Joshua there is a wonderful prediction concerning Jericho :—

"Cursed be the man before the Lord, that riseth up and buildeth this

(*h*) Gen. 12:13. (*i*) Gen. 41:29-31.

city Jericho: he shall lay the foundation thereof in his first-born, and in his youngest son shall he set up the gates of it."(*j*)

After this curse, the city of Jericho lay waste for ages; none caring to rebuild it at the expense of their first-born, and of their youngest son, until after a long succession of judges and kings, when hundreds of years had passed, Hiel the Bethelite, who lived in the days of Ahab, probably supposed that the Lord had forgotten the curse pronounced upon it by Joshua, ventured to rebuild the city; but as soon as he had laid the foundation thereof, Abiram, his first-born, died; but still persevering in the hardness of his heart, he set up the gates thereof with the loss of his youngest son, Segub, according to the word of the Lord, by Joshua. (*k*).

Elijah the prophet prophesied to Ahab that it should not rain for three years and upwards, which came to pass according to his word.

It is related of Hazael, the Syrian, who came to Elisha to inquire of the Lord concerning the king of Syria, his master, who was sick, that the prophet earnestly beholding him, burst into tears: and Hazael asked him saying, "Why weepest thou?" He then proceeded to unfold unto him the cruelties he would exercise towards Israel, which are too horrible to mention here, lest in so doing I might offend the delicate ear. Hazael, astonished to hear these things predicted concerning himself, which at that time filled him with horror, exclaimed with surprise, "But what! is thy servant a dog, that he should do this great thing?" And he said, "The Lord hath shewed me that thou shalt be king over Syria." It was all afterwards minutely fulfilled.

In the Second Chronicles, twenty-first chapter, it is written that there came a writing to Jehoram, from Elijah, which, after stating the great wickedness of which he had been guilty, in turning to idolatry and also murdering his brethren of his father's house, who were better than himself, proceeds thus:

"Behold, with a great plague will the Lord smite thy people, and thy children, and thy wives, and all thy goods: and thou shalt have great sickness by disease of thy bowels, until thy bowels fall out by reason of thy sickness day by day." (*l*)

In the same chapter it is written that the Philistines and Arabians came against him, and took his wives and children, and goods captive; and after all this, the Lord smote him in his bowels with an incurable disease, and his bowels fell out by reason of his sickness, so he died of sore disease.

(*j*) Joshua 6:26. (*k*) See 1 Kings 16:34. (*l*) 2 Chron. 21:15, 10.

We might fill a volume with instances of a similar kind, dispersed through the historical part of the Scriptures; but we forbear in order to hasten to a fuller examination of the books of the Jewish prophets. We shall trace them in their fulfillment upon Jerusalem, Babylon, Tyre, Egypt, and numerous other nations.

Babylon, the most ancient and renowned city of the world, was pleasantly situated on the banks of a majestic river that flowed through the plains of Shinar, near where the tower of Babel once stood. It was laid out four square, and surrounded with a wall upwards of three hundred feet high, and sixty miles in circumference; having an hundred gates of brass, with bars of iron: twenty-five gates on each side, which opened to streets running through the city, a distance of fifteen miles; thus forming the whole city into exact squares of equal size. In the midst of these squares were beautiful gardens adorned with trees and walks, and diversified with flowers of varied hue; while the houses were built upon the borders of the squares directly fronting on the streets. In the midst of this city sat Nebuchadnezzar, enthroned in royal splendor and magnificence, and swaying his sceptre over all the kingdoms of the world; when it pleased God in a vision of the night to raise the dark curtain of the future, and to present before him at one view the history of the world, even down to the consummation of all things. Behold a great image stood before him, whose head was of fine gold, his breast and arms of silver; his belly and thighs of brass, his legs of iron, his feet and toes part of iron and part of clay. He beheld, till a stone was cut out without hands, which smote the image upon the feet, which were part of iron and part of clay, and brake them in pieces; then was the iron, the brass, the silver and the gold, broken in pieces together, and became as the chaff of the summer threshing floor, and the wind carried them away, and there was no place found for them; but the stone which smote the image became a great mountain, and filled the whole earth. (*m*). When Daniel was brought before the king, to tell the dream and the interpretation, he exclaimed:

"There is a God in heaven that revealeth secrets, and maketh known to the king Nebuchadnezzar, what shall be in the latter days." (*n*).

After telling the dream, Daniel said:

"Thou, O king art a king of kings: for the God of heaven hath given thee a kingdom, power, and strength and glory. And wheresoever the children of men dwell, the beasts of the field and the fowls of heaven hath he given

(*m*) See Daniel 2: 31-35. (*n*) Daniel 2: 28.

into thine hand, and hath made thee ruler over them all. Thou art this head of gold. And after thee shall arise another kingdom inferior to thee, and another third kingdom of brass, which shall bear rule over all the earth. And the fourth kingdom shall be strong as iron: forasmuch as iron breaketh in pieces and subdueth all things: and as iron that breaketh all these, shall it break in pieces and bruise. And whereas thou sawest the feet and toes, part of potter's clay, and part of iron, the kingdom shall be divided; but there shall be in it the strength of the iron, forasmuch as thou sawest the iron mixed with miry clay. And as the toes of the feet were part of iron, and part of clay, so the kingdom shall be partly strong, and partly broken. And whereas thou sawest iron mixed with miry clay, they shall mingle themselves with the seed of men; but they shall not cleave one to another, even as iron is not mixed with clay. And in the days of these kings shall the God of heaven set up a kingdom, which shall never be destroyed: and the kingdom shall not be left to other people, but it shall break in pieces and consume all these kingdoms, and it shall stand forever. Forasmuch as thou sawest that the stone was cut out of the mountain without hands, and that it break in pieces the iron, the brass, the clay, the silver, and the gold; the great God hath made known to the king what shall come to pass hereafter: and the dream is certain, and the interpretation thereof sure." (*o*).

In this great view of the subject, we have presented before us in succession: first, the kingdom of Nebuchadnezzar; second, the Medes and Persians, who took Babylon from Belshazzar, and reigned over all the earth; third, the Greeks under Alexander, who conquered the world, and reigned in the midst of Babylon; fourth, the Roman Empire, which subdued all things; fifth, its division into Eastern and Western empires, and its final breaking or subdivision into the various kingdoms of modern Europe, represented by the feet and toes, part of iron and part of clay; and lastly, we have presented before us an entire new kingdom, organized by the God of heaven in the last days, or during the reign of these kings, represented by the feet and toes. This last kingdom is never to change masters, like all the kingdoms which have gone before it. It is never to be left to other people. It is to break in pieces all these kingdoms, and stand forever. Many suppose that this last kingdom alluded to, was the kingdom of God which was organized in the days of Christ or his apostles, but it is a very erroneous idea, for the kingdom of God set up in the days of Christ or his apostles, did not break in pieces any of the kingdoms of the world; it was itself warred against and overcome, in fulfillment of these words of Daniel:

"I beheld, and the same horn made war with the Saints, and prevailed against them; until the Ancient of days came, and judgment was given to the Saints of the Most High; and the time came that the Saints possessed the kingdom; * * * and the kingdom and dominion, and the

(*o*) Dan. 2:37-45.

greatness of the kingdom under the whole heaven shall be given to the people of the Saints of the Most High, whose kingdom is an everlasting kingdom, and all dominions shall serve and obey him." (*p*)

John said:—

"And it was given unto him to make war with the Saints, and to overcome them: and power was given him over all kindreds, and tongues, and nations." (*q*)

In fulfillment of these sayings, power has been given to the authorities of the earth, to kill the apostles and inspired men; until if any remained they were banished from among men, or forced to retire to the desolate islands, or the dens and caves and mountains of the earth: being men of whom the world was not worthy; while at the same time, many false prophets and teachers were introduced in their place, whom men heaped to themselves, because they would not endure sound doctrine. In this way the kingdom of God became *disorganized* and *lost* from among men, and the doctrines and churches of men instituted in its place. But we design to write more fully on the subject of the kingdom of God. Suffice it to say, that the kingdom spoken of by Daniel, is something to be organized in the last days by the God of heaven himself, without the aid of human institutions, or the precepts of men, and when organized it will never cease to roll; all the powers of earth and hell will not impede its progress, until at length the Ancient of days shall sit, and the Lord Jesus will come in the clouds of heaven, with power and great glory, as the King of kings, and Lord of lords, and destroy all these kingdoms, and give the kingdom and the greatness of the kingdom, under the whole heaven to the Saints. Then there will be but one Lord, and his name one, and He shall be king over all the earth.

We will now return to Nebuchadnezzar, whom the Lord, by the mouth of Jeremiah, calls "his servant, to execute his judgments upon the nations." It seems that the Lord exalted this great man, and made him a king of kings, and lord of lords, arming him with his own sword, and clothing him with power and authority, for the express purpose of executing his judgments, and scourging and humbling all the nations of the earth. Jeremiah, in his twenty-fifth chapter says, that the Lord proposed to bring Nebuchadnezzar and his army against Jerusalem, and against all the nations round about, that He might bring them to desolation and captivity for seventy years; and after seventy years, He would turn and punish the king

(*p*) Dan. 7: 21, 22, 27.  (*q*) Rev. 13: 7.

of Babylon, and that nation for their iniquity. Now, who can trace the history of the fulfillment of these great events, so exactly pointed out by Isaiah, Jeremiah, and Ezekiel, and not be struck with astonishment and wonder, at the marvelous *gift of prophecy* enabling men in those days to read the history of the future, as they read the history of the past. Indeed, the reader of history in the nineteenth century, holding in his hand the history of the Babylonians, Medes and Persians, Greeks, Romans and Egyptians, together with that of the Jews, will hardly render himself more familiar with the events which transpired among those nations, than the prophets were many years previous to their accomplishment.

The Jews were reduced to subjection by Nebuchadnezzar, Jerusalem was burned, together with their temple; their princes, nobles, and people were carried to Babylon, together with all their holy things. All the particulars of this destruction and captivity were distinctly foretold by Jeremiah, and the time of its continuence, viz: seventy years. After subduing the Jews, the king of Babylon marched his army against Tyre, the city of merchants, situated at the haven of the sea, surrounded not only by the sea, but with a strong wall. So strong a hold required the utmost skill and perseverance of Nebuchadnezzar and his whole army, who labored incessantly for a long time, and at last they succeeded in taking Tyre and bringing it into captivity seventy years; after which they returned and established their city, for Jeremiah had previously foretold the reduction of Tyre; its captivity of seventy years, and its restoration at the expiration of that time. After the restoration of Tyre, the city flourished for a time, but was afterwards reduced to an entire desolation. Its ruined fragments are seen to this day in the bottom of the sea; its site has become a barren rock, only occupied by poor fishermen. All this desolation and even its present appearance and desolate and perpetual waste, were clearly pointed out by the prophets.

But when the king of Babylon had succeeded in taking Tyre; after many a bald head and peeled shoulder, caused by the hard service of his army in the siege; the Lord, by the mouth of Ezekiel, promised to give the spoils of Egypt unto him, for wages for his army, in order to pay him for the great service, wherewith he had served God against Tyre. Next, witness his war in the conquest of Egypt, and bringing it into captivity.

And finally trace him, executing the Lord's vengeance and anger against Uz, upon the kings of the Philistines, and Askelon, Azaiah, and Ekron, Edom, Moab, Ammon, and Dedan, Tems, and Buz, and the kings of Arabia, and of Zimri, and of Elam, and of all the kings of the Medes, and all the kings of the north far and near; and finally upon all the kingdoms of the world, who were to be drunken, and spew, and fall to rise no more, because of the sword which he would send among them. But, when the Lord had accomplished all his mind on these nations, he purposed in turn, to punish this great monarch, and those who succeeded him, and the city and nation over which he reigned, and finally to make it perpetual desolations, and all this in consequence of their pride and haughtiness.

In order to trace the events of the deliverance of the Jews from their seventy years' captivity and bondage, and the punishment of Babylon, another and very different character from that of Nebuchadnezzar is introduced by the prophets: one who is in scripture, termed the Lord's Anointed. He may be considered one of the most extraordinary characters that the heathen world ever produced. His mildness, his courage, his perseverance, his wonderful and speedy success, and above all, his strict obedience to the commandments of *that* God, which neither he nor his fathers had known; all go to prove that Isaiah was not mistaken, when he called him by name, as the Lord's Anointed to deliver the nations from bondage, to scourge and subdue the greatest city and monarchy that has at any time existed on the earth; and to restore the Jews, and rebuild their city and temple. Indeed, he was one of those few, which the world never produces except for extraordinary purposes. But let us hear the prophet's own description of him:

"Thus saith the Lord to his anointed, to Cyrus, whose right hand I have holden to subdue nations before him ; and I will loose the loins of kings, to open before him the two-leaved gates, and the gates shall no be shut ; I will go before thee, and make the crooked places straight : I will break in pieces the gates of brass, and cut in sunder the bars of iron : and I will give thee the treasures of darkness, and hidden riches of secret places, that thou mayest know that I, the Lord, which call thee by name, am the God of Israel. For Jacob, my servant's sake, and Israel mine elect, I have even called thee by thy name : I have surnamed thee, though thou hast not known me. I am the Lord, and there is none else, there is no God besides me : I girded thee, though thou hast not known me : that they may know from the rising of the sun, and from the west, that there is none besides me. I am the Lord and there is none else." (*r*)

(*r*) Isa. 45 : 1-6.

In the thirteenth verse, the Lord says concerning Cyrus:

"I have raised him up in righteousness, and I will direct all his ways : he shall build my city and he shall let go my captives, not for price or reward, saith the Lord of hosts."

The reader will bear in mind, that Isaiah lived one hundred years before the Jewish captivity, and one hundred and seventy years before Cyrus caused their return.

What power, but the power of God, would enable one man to call another by name, a century before his birth, and also to foretell so minutely the great and peculiar events of his life? What must have been his wonder and astonishment, when after many years of wars and commotions, during which he marched forth conquering and to conquer, gathering as a nest the riches of the nations, and encamping near the walls of the strongest hold in all the earth? He gazed upon its walls of upwards of three hundred feet in height, with its gates of brass and bars of iron: the people within feeling perfectly safe, with provisions enough to last the inhabitants of the city for several years. But turning the river Euphrates from its course, and marching under the walls of the city, in the dry bed of the river, he found himself in possession of the city without any difficulty, for Belshazzar, the king, was drinking himself drunk with his nobles and concubines, and that too from the vessels of the house of the Lord which his father had taken from Jerusalem, and his knees had already smitten together with horror, from the hand-writing on the wall, which Daniel had just been called in to interpret, giving his kingdom to the Medes and Persians. Having subdued this great monarchy, he seated himself upon the throne of kingdoms; and becoming familiar with Daniel, he was probably introduced to an acquaintance with the Jewish records, whereby the mystery would be unfolded. He could then see that God had called him by name, that the Almighty hand had directed all his work. He could then understand why the treasures of the earth poured themselves into his bosom, and why the loins of the kings had been unloosed before him, and why the gates of brass had been opened, and the bars of iron burst asunder. It was that he might know that there was a God in Israel, and none else; and that all idols were as nothing; that he might also restore the Jews, and rebuild their city and temple, and fulfill God's purposes upon Babylon. He accordingly issued his proclamation to the Jews to return, and for the nations to assist them in rebuilding, for, said he, God hath commanded me to build him an house at Jerusalem. Ezra said:

"Thus saith Cyrus king of Persia, The Lord God of heaven hath given me all the kingdoms of the earth; and he hath charged me to build him an house at Jerusalem, which is in Judah. Who is there among all this people? his God be with him, and let him go up to Jerusalem, which is in Judah, and build the house of the Lord God of Israel, (he is the God), which is in Jerusalem." (s)

What powerful argument, what mighty influence was it, which caused Cyrus to be convinced that it was the God of heaven, (who dwelt in Jerusalem, who alone was God), who had done all these things? He had not been traditioned in the belief of the true God, nor of the Holy Scriptures. Nay, he had ever been zealous in the worship of idols; it was to idols he looked for assistance in the former part of his life. I reply, it was the power of God, made manifest by prophecy and its fulfillment; not in a spiritualized sense, not in some obscure, uncertain, or dark mysterious way, which was difficult to be understood; but in positive, literal, plain demonstrations, which none could gainsay or resist.—Isaiah said that this was the object the Lord had in view, when he revealed such plainness. And Cyrus manifested that it had the desired effect. When we come to treat of that part of prophecy which yet remains to be fulfilled, we shall bring positive proof that the heathen nations of the latter days, are to be convinced in the same way that Cyrus was; that is, there are certain events plainly predicted in unfulfilled prophecies, which when fulfilled, will convince all the heathen nations of the true God, and they shall know that he hath spoken and performed it. And all the great and learned men of christendom, and all societies, who have put any other than a literal construction upon the word of prophecy, shall stand confounded, and be constrained to acknowledge that all has come to pass, even as it is written.

But to return to our research of prophecy and its fulfillment. The prophets had not only predicted the reduction of Babylon by Cyrus, but they had foretold its fate through all ages, until reduced to entire desolation, never to be inhabited, not even as a temporary residence for the wandering Arab, "neither shall the Arabian pitch his tent there." (t)

Mr. Joseph Wolfe, the celebrated Jewish Missionary, while traveling in Chaldea, enquired of the Arabs whether they pitched their tents among the ruins of Babylon, to which they

(s) Ezra 1:2, 3.   (t) See Isa. 13:20-22.

replied in the negative, declaring their fears that should they do so, Nimrod's ghost would haunt them. Thus all the predictions of the prophets concerning that mighty city have been fulfilled. Edom, also, presents a striking fulfillment of plain and pointed predictions of the prophets. These predictions were pronounced upon Edom at a time when its soil was very productive and well cultivated; and every where abounding in flourishing towns and cities. But now its cities have become heaps of desolate ruins, only inhabited by the cormorant, bittern, and by wild beasts, serpents, etc., and its soil has become barren; the Lord has cast upon it the line of confusion, and the stones of emptiness, and it has been waste from generation to generation, in express fulfillment of the word of prophecy.

We now notice the vision of Daniel, concerning the ram and the goat, in the eighth chapter of Daniel. The reader will do well to read the whole chapter, but we more particularly notice the interpretation, as it was given him by Gabriel, as recorded from the nineteenth to the twenty-fifth verses.

"And he said, Behold, I will make thee know what shall be in the last end of the indignation: for at the time appointed the end shall be. The ram which thou sawest having two horns are the kings of Media and Persia. And the rough goat is the king of Grecia: and the great horn that is between his eyes is the first king. Now that being broken, whereas four stood up for it, four kingdoms shall stand up out of the nation, but not in his power. And in the latter time of their kingdom, when the transgressors are come to the full, a king of fierce countenance, and understanding dark sentences shall stand up. And his power shall be mighty, but not by his own power: and he shall destroy wonderfully, and shall prosper, and practice, and shall destroy the mighty and the holy people. And through his policy also he shall cause craft to prosper in his hand: and he shall magnify himself in his heart, and by peace shall destroy many: he shall also stand up against the Prince of princes; but he shall be broken without hand." (*u*)

In this vision, we have first presented the Medes and Persians, as they were to exist, until they were conquered by Alexander the Great. Now it is known that this empire waxed exceedingly great for some time after the death of Daniel, pushing its conquests westward, northward and southward, so that none could stand before it; until Alexander, the king of Grecia, came from the west, with a small army of chosen men, and attacked the Persians upon the bank of the river, plunging his horse in, and his army following, they crossed and attacked the Persians, who stood to oppose them on the bank, with many times their number; but notwithstanding their number, and

(*u*) Dan. 8:19-25.

their advantage of the ground, they were totally routed; and the Grecians proceeded to overrun, and subdue the country, beating the Persians in a number of pitched battles, until they were entirely subdued. It is also known that Alexander, king of Greece, went forth from nation to nation, subduing the world before him, until having conquered the world, he died at Babylon, at the age of thirty-two years. And thus when he had waxed strong, the great horn was broken, and for it came up four notable ones toward the four winds of heaven. His kingdom was divided among four of his generals, who never attained unto his power. In the latter time of their kingdom, when the transgression of the Jewish nation was come to the full, the Roman power destroyed the Jewish nation, took Jerusalem, caused the daily sacrifice to cease; and afterwards destroyed the mighty and holy people, that is, the apostles and primitive christians, who were slain by the authorities of Rome.

Now let me inquire; does the history of these United States give a plainer account of past events, than Daniel did of events that were then future; some of them reaching down the stream of time, for several hundred years, unfolding events which no human sagacity could possibly have foreseen? Man, by his own sagacity, may accomplish many things; he may plow the trackless ocean without wind or tide in his favor; he may soar aloft amid the clouds without the aid of wings; he may traverse the land with astonishing velocity without the aid of beasts; or he may convey his thoughts to his fellows by the aid of letters; or by the help of science, to the ends of the earth in a second of time. But there is a principle he can never attain; no, not even by the wisdom of ages combined; money will not purchase it; it comes from God only, and is bestowed upon man as a free gift. The prophet said to the idols, "*Show the things that are to come hereafter, that we may know ye are gods.*" (*v*).

These prophecies were literally fulfilled in relation to Jesus Christ. Behold, said the prophet, "A virgin shall conceive and bear a son." Bethlehem was to be the place of his birth; and Egypt, where he sojourned with his parents, the place out of which he was to be called, He turned aside to Nazareth, for it was written, "he shall be called a Nazarene." He rode into Jerusalem upon a colt, the foal of an ass, for the prophet had said:

(*v*) Isa. 41 : 23.

"Behold thy King cometh unto thee: he is just and having salvation; lowly, and riding upon an ass, and upon a colt the foal of an ass." (*w*).

Precisely as the prophets foretold, he was afflicted and despised; a man of sorrows, and acquainted with grief; led as a lamb to the slaughter, and like a sheep dumb before his hearers, so he opened not his mouth. In his humiliation his judgment was taken away; and who shall declare his generation, for his life was taken from the earth. He was wounded for our transgressions, and by his stripes we are healed. He was numbered with transgressors. He made his grave with the rich. Not a bone of him was broken; they divided his raiment; cast lots for his vesture; gave him gall and vinegar to drink; betrayed him for thirty pieces of silver; and finally, when it was finished, he rested in the tomb until the third day, and then rose triumphant without seeing corruption. (*x*).

Now, kind reader, if you had walked up and down with our dear Redeemer during his whole sojourn in the flesh, and taken pains to record the particular circumstances of his life and death, as they occurred from time to time, your history would not be a plainer one, than the prophets gave of him, hundreds of years before he was born. There is one thing we do well to notice, concerning the manner in which the apostles interpreted prophecy, and that is this: they quoted it, and recorded its *literal* fulfillment. By pursuing this course, they were enabled to bring it home to the hearts of the people in the Jewish synagogues, with such convincing proof, that they were constrained to believe the supposed imposter whom they had crucified was the Messiah. If they had rendered a spiritualizing or uncertain application, like the teachers of the present day, all would have been uncertainty and doubt, and demonstration would have vanished from the earth.

Having taken a view of the old Testament prophets, concerning prophecy and its fulfillment, and having shown clearly, that nothing but a literal fulfillment was intended, the objector may enquire whether the same mode will apply to the predictions contained in the New Testament? We therefore present a few important instances of prophecy, and its fulfillment; from the New Testament, after which we shall be prepared to examine the numerous prophecies which are still unfulfilled. One of the most remarkable prophecies of the Savior is recorded as follows:

"And when ye shall see Jerusalem compassed with armies, then know that the desolasion thereof it nigh. Then let them which are in Judea

(*w*) Zech. 9:9. (*x*) See Isa. 53.

flee to the mountains; and let them which are in the midst of it depart out; and let not them that are in the countries enter thereinto. For these be the days of vengeance, that all things which are written may be fulfilled. But wo unto them that are with child, and to them that give suck in those days, for there shall be great distress in the land, and wrath upon this people. And they shall fall by the edge of the sword, and shall be led away captive into all nations: and Jerusalem shall be trodden down of the Gentiles, until the time of the Gentiles be fulfilled." (*y*)

This prophecy involves the fate of Jerusalem and the temple, and the whole Jewish nation for at least eighteen hundred years. About the year seventy, the Roman army compassed Jerusalem. The disciples remembered the warning which had been given them by their Lord and Master, forty years before, and fled to the mountains. The city of Jerusalem was taken, after a long and tedious siege, in which the Jews suffered the extreme of famine, pestilence, and the sword; filling houses with the dead, for the want of a place to bury them, while women ate their own children for the want of all things. In this struggle there perished in Jerusalem near one million and a half of Jews, besides those taken captive. Their city laid waste, their temple destroyed, and the miserable remnant dispersed abroad into all the nations of the earth: in which situation they have continued ever since, being driven from one nation to another, often falsely accused of the worst of crimes, for which they were banished, and their goods confiscated. Indeed they have been mostly accounted as outlaws among the various nations; the soles of their feet have found no rest, and they have been a hiss and a by-word; and the people have said, "these are the people of the Lord, and are gone forth out of his land."

During all this time the Gentiles have possessed the land of Canaan, and trodden under foot the holy city, where their forefathers worshiped the Lord. In this long captivity the Jews have never lost sight of the promises respecting their return. Their eyes have watched and failed with longing for the day when they might possess again that blessed inheritance, bequeathed to their forefathers; when they might rear again their city and temple and re-establish their priesthood, and worship as in days of old. Indeed, they have made several attempts to return, but were always frustrated in all their attempts, for it was an unalterable decree, that Jerusalem should be trodden down of the Gentiles, until the time of the Gentiles should be fulfilled. On the subject of this long dispersion, Moses and the prophets have written very plainly; indeed, Moses even

(*y*) Luke 21: 20-24.

mentioned the particulars of their eating their children secretly in the siege, and in the straitness wherewith their enemies should besiege them in all their gates. Whoever will read Deuteronomy twenty-eighth chapter, will read the history of what has befallen the Jews, which was foretold by Moses, with all the clearness that characterizes the history of past events, thousands of years before its accomplishment. A prophet named Agabus,

"Took Paul's girdle and bound his own hands and feet, and said, Thus saith the Holy Ghost, So shall the Jews at Jerusalem bind the man that owneth this girdle, and shall deliver him into the hands of the Gentiles." (z)

The fulfillment of this prediction is too well known to need any description. We therefore proceed to notice a prophecy of Paul, recorded in 2 Tim. 4: 3, 4:

"For the time will come when they will not endure sound doctrine; but after their own lusts shall they heap to themselves teachers having itching ears; and they shall turn away their ears from the truth, and shall be turned unto fables." (a)

This prophecy has been fulfilled to the very letter; for it applies to every religious teacher, who has arisen from that day unto the present, except those commissioned by direct *revelation* and *inspired* by the *Holy Ghost*. But to convince the reader of its full accomplishment, we need only point to the numberless priests of the day who preach for hire, and divine for money, and who receive their authority from their fellow man; and as to fables to which they are turned, we need only to mention the spiritualizings and private interpretations, which salute our ears, from almost every religious press and pulpit.

There is another prophecy of Paul well worth attention, as illustrative of the times in which we live. It is as follows:

"This know also, that in the last days perilous times shall come. For men shall be lovers of their own selves, covetous, boasters, proud, blasphemers, disobedient to parents, unthankful, unholy, without natural affection, truce-breakers, false accusers, incontinent, fierce, despisers of those that are good, traitors, heady, high-minded, lovers of pleasure more than lovers of God; having a form of godliness, but denying the power thereof: from such turn away." (b).

From the last verse of this quotation, we learn to our *astonishment*, that this awful *wickedness* applies to *professors* of *religion* ONLY; that is, this would be the character of the (so-called) Christian part of community in the last days. Do not startle kind reader, we do not make the application without

(z) Acts 21:11.  (a) 2 Tim. 3:3, 4.  (b) 2 Tim. 3:1-5.

*positive* proof to the point, for remember non-professors have no form of godliness, but those ungodly characters spoken of were to have a form of godliness, denying the power thereof. But if you doubt Paul's testimony on the subject, look around you, examine for yourselves. "By their fruits you shall know them." My heart is pained while I write. Alas, has it come to this; has the Spirit of truth removed the vail of obscurity from the last days, only to present us with a vision of a fallen people; an apostate church, full of all manner of abominations, and even despising those who are good; while they themselves, have nothing left but the form of godliness, denying the power of God, that is, setting aside the direct inspiration, and supernatural gifts of the Spirit, which are always in the church of Christ? Was it for this only that the Holy Spirit opened to the view of holy men the events of unborn time, enabling them to gaze upon the opening glories of the latter days? O ye prophets and apostles, ye holy men of old, what have ye done if you stop here; if your prophetic vision only extended down the stream of time, to the present year? Alas! you have filled our minds with sorrow and despair. You have left the Jews wandering in sorrow and darkness, far from all their hearts hold most dear on earth, their land a desolation, and their city and temple in ruins, and they without the knowledge of the true Messiah. The Gentiles, after partaking of the root and fatness of the tame olive tree, having fallen, after the same example of unbelief, are left without fruit, dead, plucked up by the roots, with nought but a form of godliness, while the power that characterized the ancient church, has fled from among men.

---

## CHAPTER II.

#### ON THE FULFILLMENT OF UNFILLED PROPHECIES.

Having made the discovery, and produced sufficient proof, that the prophecies, thus far, have been LITERALLY fulfilled, we hope the reader will not lose sight of the same rule with regard to those which are unfulfilled. And while we stand upon the threshold of futurity with the wonders of unborn time about to open to our view, presenting before our astonished vision the most mighty and majestic scenes, the most astonishing revelations, the most extraordinary destructions, as well as the most miraculous displays of the power and majesty of Jehovah, in his great restoration of his long dispersed covenant people, from the four quarters of the earth; I say, as the scenes are about to open to our view, let us bow before the great I AM, in the name of Jesus, and pray in faith for his Spirit to enlarge our hearts, and enlighten our minds, that we may understand and believe all that is written, however miraculous it may be. But O, kind reader, whoever you are, if you are not prepared for persecution, if you are unprepared to have your name cast out as evil, if you cannot bear to be called a knave, an imposter, or madman, or one that hath a devil; or if you are bound by the creeds of men, to believe just so much and no more, you had better stop here; for if you were to believe the things written in the Bible, that are yet to transpire, you will be under the necessity of believing miracles, signs and wonders, revelations, and manifestations of the power of God, even beyond any thing that any former generation has witnessed; yes, you will believe that the waters will be divided, and Israel go through dry shod, as they journey to their own land, as they did in the days of Moses; for no man ever understandingly believed the Bible, without believing and expecting such glorious events in the latter days. And I will now venture to say, that a believer in the Bible, would be a person that very few men, comparatively, have ever seen in this generation, with all its boasted religion. For there is great difference in believing the book to be true when shut, and believing the things therein written. It is now considered a great disgrace not to believe the Bible when *shut;* but whosoever tries the experiment, will find that it is held to be a greater disgrace to believe that the things therein written will surely come to pass. Indeed, it is our firm belief in, and careful teaching of the things written in the Bible, which has been one great cause of the persecution we suffer; for, if the prophecies were understood by the people, according to their fulfillment, it would blow to the four winds every religious craft in christendom, and cause the kingdom of Christ to arise upon their ruins, while the actual *knowledge* of the *truth* would cover the earth as the waters do the sea.

Having said so much by way of caution, if there are any of my readers so bold, and regardless of consequenses, as to dare with me, to gaze upon the future, we will commence with Isaiah.

"And it shall come to pass in that day, that the Lord shall set his hand again the second time to recover the remnant of his people which shall be left, from Assyria, and from Egypt, and from Pathros, and from Cush, and from Elam, and from Shinar, and from Hamath, and from the islands of the sea. And he shall set up an ensign for the nations and shall assemble the outcasts of Israel, and gather together the dispersed of Judah from the four corners of the earth. * * * * And the Lord shall utterly destroy the tongue of the Egyptian sea, and with his mighty wind shall he shake his hand over the river, and smite it in the seven streams, and make men go over dry shod. And there shall be an highway for the remnant of his people, which shall be left from Assyria; like as it was to Israel in the day that he came up out of the land of Egypt." (c)

Here you behold an ensign to be reared for the nations; not only for the dispersed of Judah, but the outcasts of Israel. The Jews are called dispersed, because they are scattered among the nations; but the ten tribes are called outcasts, because they are cast out from the knowledge of the nations, in a land by themselves. Now the reader will bear in mind, that the ten tribes have not dwelt in the land of Canaan, since they were led captive by Shalmanezer, king of Assyria. We have also presented before us in the fifteenth verse the marvelous power of God, which will be displayed in the destruction of a small branch of the Red Sea; and also the dividing of the seven streams of some river; and causing men to go over dry shod: and lest any should not understand it *literally*, the fifteenth verse says:

"There shall be an highway for the remnant of his people, which shall be left from Assyria, LIKE AS *it was to Israel, in the day that he came up out of the land of Egypt.*" (d)

Now we have only to ask whether in the days of Moses, the Red Sea was *literally* divided, or whether it was only a figure? For as it was then, so it shall be again. And yet we are told by modern divines, that the days of miracles have gone forever: and those who believe in miracles in our day, are counted as imposters, or at least poor ignorant fanatics, and the public are warned against them as false teachers, who would if possible deceive the very elect. On the subject of this restoration, the prophets have spoken so fully and so repeatedly, that we can only notice a few of the most striking instances, which will go to show the particular circumstances and incidents attending it, and the manner and means of its accomplishment. Jeremiah says:

"Therefore behold, the days come, saith the Lord, that it shall no more be said, The Lord liveth, that brought up the children of Israel out

(c) **Isaiah 11:11, 12, 15, 16.** (d) **Isaiah 11:15.**

of the land of Egypt; but, the Lord liveth that brought up the children of Israel from the land of the north, and from all the lands whither he had driven them; and I will bring them again into their land that I gave unto their fathers. Behold, I will send for many fishers, and they shall fish them; and after I will send for many hunters, and they shall hunt them from every mountain, and from every hill, and out of the holes of the rocks." (*e*)

It has ever been the case with Israel, when they wished to express the greatness of their God, to say, "the Lord liveth which hath brought up our fathers out of the land of Egypt." This saying at once called to mind the power and miracles connected with that memorable event; and associated with it all that was great and grand, or calculated to strike the mind with awe, under a lively sense of the power of Israel's God. But something is yet to transpire which will cast into momentary forgetfulness, all the great events of that day, and the children of Israel shall know that their God liveth, by casting their minds upon events of recent date which shall have transpired, still more glorious and wonderful than their coming out of Egypt, therefore they will exclaim, "the Lord liveth which recently brought the children of Israel from the north and from all lands whither he had driven them; and hath planted them in the land of Canaan which he gave our fathers." With this idea will be associated every display of grandeur and sublimity, of wonder and amazement, while they call to mind the revelations, the manifestations, the miracles, and the mercies displayed in bringing about this great event, in the eyes of all the nations.

In view of this, Jeremiah exclaims in the last verse of this chapter:

"Therefore behold, I will *this once* cause them to know, I will cause them to know my hand and my might; and they shall know that my name is the Lord." (*f*)

But the means made use of to bring about this glorious event, are not only in the raising of a standard, the lifting up of an ensign, so that we may know when the time is fulfilled, but fishers and hunters are to be employed to fish and hunt them from every mountain, from every hill, and out of the holes of the rocks. Let the reader mark here, that *uninspired* men were not to send *uninspired* missionaries to teach Israel several hundred different doctrines and opinions of men, and to tell them they suppose the time has about arrived for them to gather; but the God of heaven is to call men by actual

(*e*) Jer. 16: 14–16. (*f*) Jer. 16: 21.

revelation, direct from heaven, and to tell them who Israel is; who the Indians of America are, if they should be of Israel, and also where the ten tribes are, and all the scattered remnants of that long lost people. He it is who is to give them their errand and mission, and to clothe them with power from on high to execute the great work, in defiance of opposing elements and all the opposition of earth and hell combined. But, do you ask why is the Lord to commission men by actual revelation? I reply, because He has no other way of sending men in any age. "No man, [says the apostle], taketh this honor upon himself but he that is called of God, as was Aaron." Now we all acknowledge that Aaron was called by revelation.

Now the Great Jehovah never has, and never will, acknowledge the priesthood or ministry of any man, who is not called by revelation or inspired, as were men in days of old. But, says the reader, you startle me, for the whole train of modern divines profess no revelation, later than the Bible, and no direct inspiration, or supernatural gift of the Spirit. Do you cast them all off, and say they have no authority? I reply, yes, for the Bible does it, and I humbly acquiesce in the decision, as they are nowhere known in scripture, except as teachers whom the people have heaped to themselves. The word "heap" does not mean few, but many. But to prove more fully that God will give revelations in order to bring about this glorious work, we refer to Ezekiel. It reads:

"As I live, saith the Lord God, surely with a mighty hand, and with a stretched out arm, and with fury poured out, will I rule over you; and I will bring you out from the people, and will gather you out of the countries wherein ye are scattered, with a mighty hand, and with a stretched-out arm, and with fury poured out. And I will bring you into the wilderness of the people, and there will I plead with you face to face; like as I pleaded with your fathers in the wilderness of the land of Egypt, so will I plead with you, saith the Lord God. And I will cause you to pass under the rod, and I will bring you into the bond of the covenant. And I will purge out from among you the rebels, and them that transgress against me: I will bring them forth out of the country where they sojourn, and they shall not enter into the land of Israel: and ye shall know that I am the Lord." (g)

This promise begins with a double assurance; first, with an oath, as I live; second, with an assurance, surely, with a mighty hand, etc. Lest the people should misunderstand him, he exclaims: "O Lord, they say of me, doth he not speak in parables!" Here we have the children of Israel brought from

(g) Ezek. 40: 33-38.

among all nations, with a mighty hand and a stretched out arm, and with fury poured out. (O ye nations who oppose these things, beware, remember Pharaoh, and learn wisdom!) We see them brought into the wilderness of the people; and there the Lord is to plead with them, face to face, just as he did with their fathers, in the wilderness of Egypt. This pleading face to face can never be done, without revelation, and a personal manifestation as much so as in old times. Now I ask, was all His manifestations to Israel in the wilderness a mere fable, not to be understood literally? If so, this will be so too; for one will be precisely like the other, no parable but a glorious reality. He will cause them to pass under the rod, and bring them into the bond of the covenant. This brings to mind the new covenant, so often promised in the Scriptures, to be made with the house of Israel and with the house of Judah, just in time to gather them from their long dispersion. Some may suppose that the new covenant which was to gather Israel made its appearance in the days of Christ and his Apostles, but Paul in his day represents that it was an unfulfilled prophesy.

"That blindness in part is happened unto Israel, until the fullness of the Gentiles be come in. And so all Israel shall be saved; as it is written, There shall come out of Zion the Deliverer, and shall turn away ungodliness from Jacob; for this is my covenant unto them, when I shall take away their sins." (*h*)

From this we learn that Paul placed that covenant in the future, even down to the restoration of Israel in the last days, when the times of the Gentiles should be fulfilled. Then there should come a deliverer for Israel, and not before, seeing that they had rejected the first coming of that deliverer. And He himself said to the Jews,

"Behold your house is left unto you desolate. For I say unto you, Ye shall not see me henceforth, till ye shall say, Blessed is he that cometh in the name of the Lord." (*i*)

Then, and not until then, will the covenant be renewed with Israel. And even when the Apostles enquired, saying, "Wilt thou at this time restore again the kingdom to Israel?" the Savior said that it was not for them to know the times and seasons, which the father had put in his own power; but they were to receive power, and bear witness of him, etc.; as much as to say, "that work is not for you, mine Apostles to accomplish, but it shall be done in the Lord's own time, by whom he will; but go ye, and do the work I have commanded you."

(*h*) Rom. 11:25-27. (*i*) Matt. 23:38, 39.

Isaiah, in speaking of this covenant, tell us, that it should make their seed known among the Gentiles, and their offspring among the people, and cause all that see them, to acknowledge them, that they are the seed that the Lord hath blessed. (*j*)

Now we know that it is a question which can only be decided by revelation, whether the aborigines of America are the seed of Jacob or not; and there has been much controversy concerning the location of the ten tribes, and who they are; but the new covenant will reveal these things, and will leave the matter no longer in suspense; we shall then know their seed among the Gentiles, and their offspring among the people. But O, how different was the effect of the covenant made eighteen hundred years ago in its effects upon Israel; it cast them off in unbelief, and caused all that have seen them or heard of them ever since to acknowledge that they are the seed the Lord hath *cursed*. When the covenant is renewed in the last days the Lord will bring them into the bond of the covenant, by manifesting himself to them face to face. Let me inquire how does God make a covenant with the people in any age? The answer is, by communicating His will to them by actual revelation; for without this, it would be impossible to make a covenant between two parties. In order to illustrate this subject, let us bring an example and see how we make covenant with each other. For instance, a young man wishes to enter into a covenant of matrimony with a young lady; but deprive him of the privilege of revealing his mind to her, cut off all direct communication between them, and a covenant could never be made; and so it is with the Almighty. He never did enter into a covenant with his creatures, without revelations; and He never can do it. In short, whenever He made covenant with the people, where a whole people were concerned, he included in the covenant, the priesthood, offices, and authorities, together with the ordinances and blessings which pretain to His covenant; and so will He do at this time. Whenever the new covenant is established, it will organize the kingdom of God with all its offices, ordinances, gifts and blessings, as in days of old; but more of this when we come to treat of the kingdom of God. But, says the inquirer, What need have we of the renewal of a covenant which has never been broken? If the Lord made a covenant in the days of the Apostles, called a new covenant, why should that covenant still be renewed again, seeing it is in full force until it is broken by

(*j*) Isa. 61 : 8, 9.

one party or the other? This is an important inquiry, involving the fate of all Christendom in its decision; we must therefore be very careful to make the decision perfectly plain, and the proof easy to be understood. That there was a new covenant made between God and his people, in the days of Christ and His Apostles, we will not deny; and if that covenant never has been broken, it must be in force till the present day, and consequently there is no need of a new one. It therefore remains for us to prove that the covenant has been broken —completely broken, so that it is not in force, either among Jews or Gentiles, having lost its offices, authorities, powers and blessings, insomuch that they are no where to be found among men. In order to do this, we must examine what were its offices, authorities, power and blessings, and then see whether they are still known to exist.

We read taht its offices consisted of Apostles, Prophets, Evangelists, Pastors and Teachers, all inspired, and set in the Church by the Lord himself, for the edifying of the Saints, for the work of the ministry, etc. And they were to continue in the Church, wherever it was found, until they all come to the unity of the faith, and unto the measure of the stature of a man in Christ. (*k*)

Secondly, the gifts of the Spirit, which some call supernatural, were the powers and blessings which pretained to that covenant, wherever it existed, among the Jews or Gentiles, so long as the covenant was in force. Now, I would ask the whole of Christendom, or any of its sects or parties, if they have Apostles, Prophets, Evangelists, Pastors, and Teachers, inspired from on high, together with the gifts and blessings of the Holy Spirit, which pertained to the gospel covenant? If not, then the offices and power of that covenant have been lost. And it must be through the breaking of that covenant, that they were lost; for in this way the Jews lost these privileges, when they were handed to the Gentiles. And Paul told the Gentiles, in Romans eleventh chapter, than if they did not abide in his goodness, they would fall, as the Jews had done before them. But in order to prove by further demonstration, that the gospel covenant has been broken, by Jew and Gentile and all people, so as to be no longer in force, I shall quote. (*l*)

"Behold, the Lord maketh the earth empty, and maketh it waste, and turneth it upside down, and scattereth abroad the inhabitants thereof. And it shall be, as with the people, so with the priest; as with the ser-

(*k*) See Ephesians 4th chapter. (*l*) Isa. 24 : 1–6.

vant, so with his master; as with the maid, so with her mistress; as with the buyer, so with the seller; as with the lender, so with the borrower; as with the taker of usury, so with the giver of usury to him. The land shall be utterly emptied, and utterly spoiled: for the Lord hath spoken this word. The earth mourneth and fadeth away, the world languisheth and fadeth away, the haughty people of the earth do languish. The earth also is defiled under the inhabitants thereof; BECAUSE THEY HAVE TRANSGRESSED THE LAWS, CHANGED THE ORDINANCE, BROKEN THE EVERLASTING COVENANT. Therefore hath the curse devoured the earth, and and they that dwell therein are desolate; therefore the inhabitants of the earth are burned, and few men left."

In these verses we discover a like calamity awaiting priest and people, rich and poor, bond and free, insomuch that all are to be burned up but a few, and the complaint is that the earth is defiled under the inhabitants thereof, because they have transgressed the law, changed the ordinance, and broken the everlasting covenant. Now, this could not be speaking of any other than the covenant, ordinances and law of the gospel, made with the people in the days of the Apostles; because, however any former covenant may have been broken, yet all the inhabitants of the earth excepting only a few, were never destroyed by fire, for having broken any previous covenant; but this destruction is to come by fire as literally as the flood in the days of Noah; and it will consume both priests and people from the earth; and that too for having broken the covenant of the gospel, with its laws and its ordinances; or else we must get a new edition of the Bible, leaving out the twenty-fourth chapter of Isaiah.

Now, having settled this question, I trust the reader will see the need of a new covenant, in order to save the few that are not to be burned. We will therefore dismiss this subject for the present, and turn again to the subject of the gathering of Israel. You will please read Ezekiel thirty-sixth to the thirty-ninth chaper. In the thirty-sixth chapter you will discover a promise that Israel is to return from all the nations whither they have been scattered, and to be brought again to the land which God gave to their fathers. Jerusalem is to be filled with men, and the desolate cities of Judea are to be rebuilt, fenced and inhabited. The land is to be fenced, tilled and sown, insomuch, that they will say, "this land that was desolate, is become like the garden of Eden." The Lord says:—

"I the Lord build the ruined places, and plant that that was desolate, I the Lord have spoken it, and I will do it. * * * As the holy flock, as the flock of Jerusalem in her solemn feasts; so shall the waste cities be filled with flocks of men; and they shall know that I am the Lord." (*m*).

In the thirty-seventh chapter, after the vision of the dead, the prophet foretells that the two nations will become one nation upon the mountains of Israel, and one king be king to them all; and when this takes place, they are no more to be divided into two kingdoms. Moreover, the Lord's tabernacle is to be with them, and His sanctuary in the midst of them forevermore; He will forever be their God, and they shall be his people. The Lord says:—

"And the heathen shall know that I the Lord do sanctify Israel, when my sanctuary shall be in the midst of them for evermore." (*n*)

Now, it is a fact well known, that Judah and the ten tribes have never been one nation upon the mountains of Israel, since the day they were first divided into two nations.

But, when this will take place, even the very heathen are to know it, and are to be convinced of the true God, as was the case with Cyrus. Now, if the missionaries should convert the world before the Lord does this great work, then it will save the Lord the trouble of doing it in his own way, and it will save the trouble of fulfilling the prophecies, and the word of the Lord will fail, and all the world may lay hold on infidelity. Well did the Lord say, "my ways are not as your ways, nor my thoughts as your thoughts." Chapters thirty-eight and thirty-nine present us with a view of many nations, united under one great head, whom the Lord is pleased to call Gog; and being mounted on horseback, and armed with all sorts of armor, they came up against the mountains of Israel, as a cloud to cover the land; their object is to take a prey, to take away silver and gold, and cattle, and goods in great abundance.

And this is an event which is to transpire after the return of the Jews, and the rebuilding of Jerusalem; while the towns of the land of Judea are without walls, having neither bars nor gates. But while they are at the point to swollow up the Jews, and lay waste their country, behold the Lord's fury comes up in his face, a mighty earthquake is the result, insomuch that the fishes of the sea, and the fowls of the air, and all the creeping things, and all men upon the face of the earth shall fall to the ground, and every man's sword shall be against his neighbor in this army, and the Lord shall rain upon him and upon his bands, and upon the many people that are with him, an overflowing rain, great hailstones, fire and brimstone. And thus he will magnify himself, and sanctify

(*m*) Ezekiel 36 : 36–38.   (*n*) Ezekiel 37 : 28.

himself, in the eyes of many nations, and they shall know that he is the Lord; thus shall they fall upon the open field, upon the mountains of Israel, even Gog and all his army, horses horsemen; and the Jews shall go forth and gather the weapons of war, such as had staves, spears, shields and bows and arrows; and these weapons shall last the cities of Israel seven years for fuel, so that they shall cut no wood out of the forests, for they shall burn the weapons with fire; and they shall spoil those that spoiled them, and rob those that robbed them, and they shall gather gold and silver, and apparel, in great abundance. At this time, the fowls of the air, and the beasts of the field, shall have a great feast; yea, they are to eat fat until they be full, and drink blood until they be drunken. They are to eat flesh of captains, and kings, and mighty men, and all men of war. But the Jews will have a very serious duty to perform, which will take no less than seven months; namely, the burying of their enemies. They will select a place on the east side of the sea, called the Valley of the Passengers; and there shall they bury Gog, and all his multitude, and they shall call it the Valley of Hamon Gog. And the scent shall go forth, insomuhc that it shall stop the noses of the passengers; thus shall they cleanse the land. The Lord says,.

"And I will set my glory among the heathen, and all the heathen shall see my judgment that I have executed, and my hand that I have laid upon them; so the house of Israel shall know that I am the Lord their God from that day forward. And the heathen shall know that the house of Israel went into captivity for their iniquity, because they trespassed against me; therefore hid I my face from them, and gave them into the hands of their enemies, so fell they all by the sword. According to their uncleanness, and according to all their transgressions have I done unto them, and hid my face from them; therefore thus saith the Lord God, now will I bring again the captivity of Jacob, and have mercy upon the whole house of Israel, and will be jealous for my holy name; after that they have borne their shame, and all their trespasses, whereby they have trespassed against me, when they dwelt safely in their land, and none made them afraid. When I have brought them again from the people, and gathered them out of their enemies, lands, and am sanctified in them, in the eyes of many nations; then shall they know that I am the Lord their God, who caused them to be led into captivity among the heathen; but I have gathered them into their own land, and have left none of them any more there; neither will I hide my face any more from them, for I have poured out my spirit upon the house of Israel, saith the Lord God." (o)

In the foregoing quotation, we discover that the heathen are to know, that the house of Israel went into captivity for their iniquity, and are gathered again by the hand of God,

(o) Ezek. 39:21-29.

after having borne their shame for all their trespasses, and the house of Israel shall know that it was the Lord their God who caused them to be led into captivity among the heathen, and that He it was, that gathered and defended them, and He will hide His face no more from them, but will pour out his Spirit on them.

O, ye blind, ye stiff-necked, ye hard-hearted generation, with the Bible circulated among all nations. Will whole nations be so blind as to fulfill this prophecy, and not know it, until it brings destruction upon their own head? Why all this blindness? Alas! it is because of false teachers who will tell them the Bible must be spiritualized. Others declare that these prophecies can never be understood, until they are fulfilled. If this be the case, then we can never escape the judgments predicted in them, but must continue the children of darkness, until they come upon us unaware, and sweep us from the earth. Then where will be the consolation of looking back and seeing them fulfilled? But blessed be God, He has told us by the mouth of Daniel, that many shall run to and fro, and knowledge shall be increased, and that the wise shall understand. And now I ask, who are more wicked than the wilfully blind leaders of the blind, who tell us we can not understand the Scriptures?

Zechariah, in his fourteenth chapter, has told us much concerning the great battle and overthrow of the nations who fight against Jerusalem, and he has said in plain words, that the Lord should come at the time of the overthrow of that army; yes, in fact even while they are in the act of taking Jerusalem, and have already succeeded in taking one half of the city and spoiling their houses, and ravishing their women. Then the Jews behold their Messiah, suddenly standing, His feet upon the Mount of Olives, a little east of Jerusalem, to fight against those nations, and deliver the Jew. Zechariah says, the Mount of Olives shall cleave in twain, from east to west, and one half of the mountain shall remove to the north, while the other half shall fall off to the south; suddenly forming a very great valley into which the Jews shall flee for protection from their enemies, like they fled from the earthquake in the days of Uzziah, king of Judah; while the Lord will come, and all the Saints with him. Then will the Jews behold that long expected Messiah, coming in power to their deliverance, as they always looked for him. He will destroy their enemies, and deliver them from trouble at the very time when they will be in the utmost consternation, and about to be swallowed up by their enemies. But what will be their astonishment, when they see their Deliverer, and acknowledge Him as their Messiah, they discover the wounds which once pierced His hands, and feet, and side, and on inquiry at once recognize Jesus of Nazareth, the king of the Jews, the man so long rejected. Well did the prophet say, they shall mourn and weep, every family apart, and their wives apart. But, thank heaven, there will be an end to their mourning; for He will forgive their iniquities, and cleanse them from all uncleanness. Jerusalem shall be a holy city from that time forth; and all the land shall be turned as a plain from Geba to Rimmon, and shall be lifted up and inhabited in her place, and men shall dwell there, and there shall be no more utter destruction of Jerusalem, "and in that day there shall be one Lord, and his name one, and he shall be King over all the earth." John, in the eleventh chapter of Revelations, gives us many more particulars concerning this event. He informs us that after the city and temple will be rebuilt by the Jews, the Gentiles will tread it under foot, forty and two months, during which time there shall be two prophets continually prophesying, and working mighty miracles. And it seems that the Gentile army will be hindered from utterly destroying and overthrowing the city, while these two prophets continue. But after a struggle of three years and a half, they at length will succeed in destroying these two prophets, and then they will overrun much of the city. They will send gifts to each other, because of the death of the two prophets, and in the mean time they will not allow their dead bodies to be put in graves, but will suffer them to lie in the streets of Jerusalem three days and a half; during which time the armies of the Gentiles, consisting of many kindred, tongues, and nations, (passing through the city, plundering the Jews), will see their dead bodies lying in the street. But after three days and a half, (suddenly), the Spirit of life from God will enter them, and they will arise and stand upon their feet, and great fear will fall upon them that see them. And then they will hear a voice from heaven, saying, "Come up hither," and they will ascend up to heaven in a cloud, and their enemies will behold them. Then will come the shaking spoken of by Ezekiel; and the rending of the Mount of Olives, spoken of by Zechariah. John says: "The same hour there was a great earthquake, and the tenth part of the city fell; and in the earthquake were slain of men seven thousand." Then one of the next scenes which will follow, will be the sound of voices, saying,—"The kingdoms of this world are become the kingdoms of our Lord and His Christ, and He shall reign for ever and ever."

Having described the great events spoken of by these prophets: I remark, that there is no difficulty in understanding them all to be plain, and literal in their fulfillment.

Suffice it is to say, the Jews will gather home, and rebuild Jerusalem. The nations will gather against them to battle. Their armies will compass the city, and have power over it for three years and a half. Two Jewish prophets, by their mighty miracles, will keep them from utterly overcoming the Jews, until at length they will be slain; and the city will be left in a great measure to the pillage of their enemies for three days and a half; the two prophets will then rise from the dead, and ascend up into heaven. The Messiah will come, convulse the earth, overthrow the armies of the Gentiles, deliver the Jews, cleanse Jerusalem, cut off all wickedness from the earth, raise the Saints from the dead, bring them with him, and commence his reign of a thousand years; during which time His Spirit will be poured out upon all flesh; men and beasts, birds and serpents, will be harmless, and the knowledge and glory of God will cover the earth as the waters cover the sea, and the kingdom and the greatness of the kingdom under the whole heaven, will be given to the Saints of the Most High.

During the thousand years Satan will be bound, and have no power to tempt the children of men. And the earth itself will be delivered from the curse which came by reason of the fall. The rough places will become smooth; the barren desert fruitful; the mountain leveled; the valleys exalted; the thorn and thistle shall no more be found, but all the earth shall yield her increase in abundance for the Saints of God. After the thousand years are ended, then shall Satan be loosed, and go out to deceive the nations which dwell in the four quarters of the earth, to gather them, and bring them up to battle against the camp of the Saints. Then the great and last struggle will take place between God and Satan, for the empire of the earth. Satan and his army will be overthrown. And after these great events, the end of the earth, the resurrection of the wicked, and the last judgment will come. And there shall be a new earth, and a new heaven, for the former earth and the former heaven will pass away, that is, they will be changed from temporal to eternal, and made fit for the abode of immortals. Then cometh Jerusalem down from God out of heaven, having been renewed, as well as the heavens and the earth. For said he, "Behold I make all things new." This new city, placed upon the new earth, with the Lord God and the Lamb in the midst, is man's eternal abode; so after all our longings for a place "beyond the bounds of time and space," (as saith the poet), we are at last brought to our common senses, and given to understand that man is destined forever to inherit the same planet upon which he was first created; after it is redeemed, sanctified, renewed, purified and prepared as an eternal inheritance of immortal saints, with the Holy City for the capital, the throne of God in the midst for the seat of Government; and watered with a stream clear as crystal, called the Waters of Life, which will issue from the throne of Jehovah; while either side will be adorned with trees of never fading beauty.

"Blessed are they that do his commandments, that they may have right to the tree of life, and may enter in through the gates into the city." (p)

By this time we begin to understand the words of the Savior: "Blessed are the meek, for they shall inherit the earth;" and the song which John heard in heaven, which ended thus: "We shall reign on the earth."

We gather from the field of prophecy, through which we have passed, first, that that glorious day will be ushered in by the personal coming of Christ, and the resurrection of all the Saints. Second, we learn that all the wicked will be destroyed from the earth, by overwhelming judgment of God, and by fire at the time of His coming, insomuch that the earth will be cleansed by fire from its wicked inhabitants, as it was once by water; and that burning will include priests as well as people: all but few shall be burned. This burning more especially applies to the fallen church, than to the heathen or Jews, whom they are now trying to convert. Woe unto you, Gentiles, who call yourselves the people of the Lord, but have made void the law of God by your traditions; for in vain do you call, Lord, Lord, and do not the things which Jesus commands; in vain do ye worship him, teaching for doctrines the commandments of man. Behold the sword of vengeance hangs over you, and except you repent, it will soon fall upon you, and it will be more tolerable in that day for the Jews and heathen, than for you. Behold ye flatter yourselves that the glorious day, spoken of the prophets, will be ushered in by your modern inventions and pecuniary plans, which are got up in order to convert the Jews and heathen to the various sectarian creeds

(p) Revelations 22 : 14.

now existing among yourselves, and you expect when this is done, to behold a Millenium after your own hearts. But the Jews and heathen never will be converted as peoples, by any other plan than that laid down in the Bible for the great restoration of Israel. And *you yourselves* are laboring under a broken covenant, and ripening for the fire as fast as possible. But do not count me your enemy because I tell you the truth; for God is my witness that I love your souls too well to keep back any truth from you, however severe it may seem. The wounds of a friend are better than the kisses of an enemy.

Concerning the signs of the time, the inquiry often arises, when shall these things be, and what sign shall there be when these things shall come to pass? I am often asked the question whether it is near at hand; I will therefore tell you all, whereby you may know for yourselves, (and not to depend on the knowledge of others), when it is nigh, even at the doors.

Now you behold the apple tree, and all the trees, when they begin to shoot forth their leaves, ye know of your own selves that summer is nigh at hand; and so likewise when ye shall see great earthquakes, famines, pestilences, and plagues of every kind, and all things in commotion; like the sea and the waves roaring: the nations distressed with perplexity; men's hearts failing them for fear, and for looking for the things which are coming on the earth—when you see signs in the heaven above and in the earth beneath, blood, and fire, and vapor of smoke; the sun turned to darkness, the moon to blood, and the stars hurled from their courses—when you see the Jews gathering to Jerusalem, and the armies of the nations gathering against them to battle—you may know with a perfect knowledge that His coming is near, even at the doors.

"*Verily, verily,* I *say* unto you, *this* generation shall not pass away till all be fulfilled. Heaven and earth shall pass away, but my words shall not pass away" (*q*)

Whosoever will believe the words of the prophets, and the sayings of Jesus Christ, on this subject, will be convinced that all the signs of which I have spoken, are clearly pointed out as the signs of His coming. But, notwithstanding all these things are written, His coming will overtake the world unawares, as the flood did the people in the days of Noah. The reason is, they will not understand the prophets. They will not endure sound doctrine; their ears are turned away from the truth, and turned to fables, because of false teachers and the precepts of men; and what is still worse, when God

(*q*) Matt. 24 : 34, 35.

sends men with the new and everlasting covenant, and clothes them with boldness to testify of the truth, they will be treated as the servants of God have been before them by the fallen churches. Every church will cleave to its own way, and they will unite in saying, "There is no need of these new things, the good old way is right;" while at the same time they are walking in as many different ways as there are sects, and only agreed in persecuting and speaking all manner of evil against the fishers and hunters whom God shall send. But, thank heaven, there are individuals in every sect who are humbly seeking the truth, and who will know the voice of truth, and be gathered out and planted in the new and everlasting covenant, and they will be adopted into the family of Israel, and will be gathered with them, and be partakers of the same covenant of promise. Yea, as Jeremiah says,—

"The Gentiles shall come unto thee from the ends of the earth, and shall say, Surely our fathers have inherited lies, vanities, and things wherein there is no profit." (r)

But, as the Jews overlooked His first coming, by not understanding the prophets, and by concentrating their minds exclusively on His glorious coming in the last days to restore the kingdom to Israel, and avenge them of their enemies; and by this mistake were broken and scattered: so the Gentiles will overlook the prophecies concerning his second coming, by confounding them with the last judgment, which is to take place more than a thousand years afterward. But this fatal mistake, instead of causing the Gentiles to be broken and scattered, will cause them to be ground to powder.

O! my brethren according to the flesh, my soul mourns over you; and had I a voice like a trumpet, I would cry, awake, awake, and arouse from your slumbers, for the time is fulfilled, your destruction is at the door:—

"For I have heard from the Lord God of hosts, a consumption, even determined upon the whole earth." (s)

Prepare to meet your God! And again, awake, O! house of Israel, and lift up your head, for your redemption draweth nigh: Yea, depart ye, depart ye, go ye out from hence, gather home from your long dispersion; rebuild your cities; yea, go ye out from the nations, from one end of heaven to the other; but let not your flight be in haste, for the Lord shall go before you, and the God of Israel shall be your rearward. And finally, I would say to all, both Jews and Gentiles, repent ye, repent

(r) Jeremiah 16 : 19.  (s) Isaiah 28 : 22.

ye, for the great day of the Lord is at hand. For if I, who am a man, do lift up my voice, and call upon you to repent, and ye hate me, what will ye say when the day cometh, when the thunders shall utter their voices to the ends of the earth, speaking to the ears of all that live, saying, "Repent, and prepare for the great day of the Lord." Yea, again, when the lightnings shall streak forth from the east unto the west, and shall utter forth their voices unto all that live, and make the ears of all that hear to tingle, saying these words: "Repent ye, for the great day of the Lord is come." And again, the Lord shall utter his voice out of the heaven, saying,—

"Harken, O ye nations of the earth, and hear the words of that God who made you; O ye nations of the earth, how often would I have gathered you together as a hen gathereth her chickens under her wings, but ye would not."

"How often have I called upon you by the mouth of my servants, and by the ministering of angels, and by mine own voice, and by the voice of thunderings, and by the voice of lightnings, and by the voice of tempests, and by the voice of earthquakes and great hailstorms, and by the voice of famine, and pestilences of every kind, and by the great sound of a trumpet, and by the voice of judgments, and by the voice of mercy, all the day long, and by the voice of glory and honor, and the riches of eternal life; and would have saved you with an everlasting salvation, but you would not."

"Behold the day has come, when the cup of the wrath of mine indignation is full."

---

## CHAPTER III.

### THE KINGDOM OF GOD.

"Seek first the kingdom of God." This was the command of the Savior while He was on the earth, teaching the children of men.

Having taken a general view of the fulfilled and unfulfilled prophecies, we will now search for the kingdom of God. I would again ask the reader if he is prepared to sacrifice every thing, even his good name, and his life itself, if necessary, as a sacrifice for the truth; for if he should once get a view of the kingdom of God, he will be so delighted that he will never rest satisfied without becoming a citizen of the same. It will be so unlike every other system of religion now on earth, that he will be astonished that any person with the Bible in his hand, should ever have mistaken any of the systems of men, for the kingdom of God. There are certain powers, privileges and blessings, pertaining to the kingdom of God, which are found in no other kingdom, nor enjoyed by any other people. By these things it was always distinguished from all other kingdoms and systems, insomuch that the inquirer who is seeking the kingdom of God, being once acquainted with these peculiarites concerning it, need never mistake; nor be at a loss to know when he has found it. Before we proceed any farther in our research, let us agree upon the meaning of the term, or the sense in which we will use it; for some apply this term to the kingdom of glory above, and some to the individual enjoyments of their own souls, while others apply it to His organized government on the earth. Now when we speak of the kingdom of God, we wish to be understood as speaking of His organized government on the earth.

Let us consider: What is a kingdom? I reply, that four things are requisite to constitute any kingdom, in heaven or on earth: namely, first, a king; secondly, commissioned officers duly qualified to execute his ordinances and laws; thirdly, a code of laws by which the citizens are governed; and fourthly, subjects who are governed. Now, where these exist in their proper order and regular authority, there is a kingdom; but where either of these ceases to exist, there is a disorganization of the kingdom, consequently an end of the kingdom, until it is reorganized after the same manner as before. Now in this respect, the kingdom of God is like all other kingdoms; wheresoever we find officers duly commissioned and qualified by the Lord Jesus, together with his ordinances and laws existing in purity, unmixed with any precepts or commandments of men, there the kingdom of God exists; and there his power is manifest, and his blessings enjoyed as in days of old.

We shall now take a view of the setting up of the kingdom of God in the days of the ancient apostles. The first intimation of its near approach was by an angel to Zechariah, promising him a son, who should go before the king to prepare his way. The next manifestation was to Mary, and then to Joseph, by an holy angel, promising the birth of the Messiah; while at the same time the Holy Ghost manifested unto Simeon that he should not die until he had seen the Savior. Thus, all these, together with the shepherds and the wise men from the east, began to rejoice with a joy unspeakable and full of glory, while the world around them knew not the occasion of their joy. After these things, all seemed to rest in silent expectation, until John had grown to manhood. "In those days came John the Baptist, preaching in the wilderness of Judea and saying, Repent ye for the kingdom of heaven is at hand." He baptized unto repentance, telling them plainly that their king was already standing among them, and would set up his kingdom. And while he yet ministered, the Messiah came, and was baptized and sealed with the Spirit of God, which rested upon Him in the form of a dove; and soon after he began the same proclamation as John, saying, "Repent ye, for the kingdom of heaven is at hand." Soon after, he chose twelve apostles and sent them forth into all the cities of Judea, with the same proclamation, "the kingdom of heaven is at hand;" and after them He sent seventy elders, and another seventy, with the same news, so that all might be well warned and prepared for a kingdom, which was soon to be organized amongst them. But when these things had produced the desired effect, in causing a general expectation, more especially in the hearts of his disciples, who daily expected to triumph over their persecutors, by the coronation of this glorious personage, while they themselves were hoping for a reward for all their toil and sacrifices for his sake, by being exalted to dignity near his person, what must have been their disappointment, when they saw their king taken and crucified, being mocked, derided, ridiculed, and finally overcome and triumphed over both by Jew and Gentile? They would gladly have died in battle to have placed him upon the throne; but tamely to submit without a struggle, to give up all their expectations, and sink in despair, from the highest pitch of enthusiasm to the lowest degradation, was more than they could well endure. They shrunk back in sorrow, and turned every man unto his net, or to their several occupations, supposing that all was lost; probably with reflections like these: "Is this the result of all our labors? Was it for this we forsook all wordly objects, our friends, our houses and lands, suffering persecution, hunger, fatigue, and disgrace? We trusted that it would have been He who would have delivered Israel; but alas, they have killed him, and all is lost. For three years we have awakened a general expectation through all Judea, by telling them that the kingdom of heaven was at hand, but now our king is dead, how shall we dare to look the people in the face?" With these reflections, each pursuing his own course, all was again turned to silence, and the voice had ceased to be heard in Judea, crying, "Repent ye for the kingdom of heaven is at hand." Jesus slept in the arms of death; a great stone with the seal of state secured the tomb where he lay, while the Roman guard stood in watchful silence, to see that all was kept secure, when suddenly from the regions of glory, a mighty angel descended, at whose presence the soldiers fell back as dead men, while he rolled the stone from the door of the sepulchre, and the Son of God awoke from his slumbers, burst the bands of death, and soon after appearing to Mary, He sent her to the disciples with the joyful news of His resurrection, and appointed a place to meet them. After seeing Him, all their sorrow was turned into joy, and all their former hopes were suddenly revived. They had no longer to cry, "The kingdom of heaven is at hand," but were to tarry at Jerusalem, until they should be endowed with power from on high. Then the kingdom was established, and they unlocked the door of the kingdom, and adopted strangers and foreigners into it as legal citizens, by administering certain laws and ordinances, which were invariably the laws of adoption; without which no man could ever become a citizen. After His resurrection, He came to His disciples and gave them their authority, saying unto them:

"Go ye into all the world, and preach the gospel to every creature. He that believeth and is baptized shall be saved, but he that believeth not shall be damned: and these signs shall follow them that believe: in my name shall they cast out devils; they shall speak with new tongues; they shall take up serpents; and if they drink any deadly thing it shall not hurt them; they shall lay hands on the sick and they shall recover;" (*t*).

Now, I wish the reader would never forget this commission, until he understands it, because when he understands it, he never need mistake the kingdom of God, but will at once discover those peculiarities, which were forever to distinguish it from all other kingdoms or religious systems on earth; and lest he should misunderstand it, we will analyze it, and look at each part carefully in its own proper light. First, they were to preach the gospel, (or in other words, the glad tidings of a crucified and risen Redeemer), to all the world. Secondly, he that believeth and is baptized, shall be saved. Thirdly, he that did not believe what they preached should be damned; and fourthly, these signs should follow them that believe: first, they are to cast out devils; second, to speak with new

(*t*) Mark 16 : 15-18.

tongues; third, to take up serpents; fourth, if they drink any deadly thing, it shall not hurt them; fifth, they were to lay hands on the sick, and they should recover.

If he that believeth and is baptized *in our day* shall be saved, and if he that believeth not *in our day* shall be damned, then these signs follow them that believe *in our day*. That commission contains the *unchangeable* conditions of salvation, for there is no provision made in the scriptures for a change in those conditions, or in the blessings which were promised by the Savior to those who should obey his gospel.

Now it is willful blindness, or ignorance of the English language, that has ever caused any misunderstanding here. For some do tell us that those signs were only to follow the apostles; and others tell us that they were only to follow believers of that age. But Christ places the preaching, the believing, the salvation, and the signs that were to follow, all on an equal footing. Where one was limited the other must be; where one ceased, the other did. If the language limits these signs to the apostles, it limits faith and salvation also to them. If no others were to have these signs follow them, then no others were to believe, and no others were to be saved. If this commission limits these signs to the first age or ages of Christianity, then it limits salvation to the first ages of Christianity; for one is precisely as much limited as the other; and where one is in force the other is, and where one ends the other must. And as well might we say that preaching of the gospel is no longer needed; faith is no longer needed; salvation is no longer needed; they were only given at first to establish the gospel, as to say these signs are no longer necessary, they were only given at first to establish the gospel. But, says the astonished reader, have not these signs ceased from among men? I reply, prove that they have ceased, and it will prove that the gospel has ceased to be preached, and that men have ceased to believe and be saved, and that the world is without the kingdom of God; or else it will prove that Jesus Christ was an impostor, and his promises of no effect.

Now, having analyzed and understood this commission, let us still pursue the subject of the organization of the kingdom of God, in the days of the apostles. The Savior having given them their authority, commanded them to tarry and not undertake their mission, until they were endowed with power from on high. But why this delay? Because no man was ever qualified, or ever will be, to preach the gospel, and teach all things whatsoever Jesus commanded them, without the Holy Ghost; and a very different Holy Ghost too, from the one now enjoyed by men who are not inspired, for the Holy Ghost of which Jesus spake would guide into all truth, bring all things to remembrance, whatsoever he had said unto them, and show them things to come, and enable them to speak in other tongues. Now a man who preaches needs the Holy Ghost very much; first, to guide into all truth, that he may know what to teach; second, to strengthen his memory, lest he might neglect to teach some of the things which were commanded them; and third, he needs it to know things to come, (and that would constitute him a prophet), that he might forewarn his hearers of approaching danger. From this, the reader may see how careful Jesus was, that none should preach his gospel without the Holy Ghost. He may also learn how different the Spirit of truth is, from the spirits now abroad in the earth, deceiving the world, under the name of the Holy Ghost. If the churches of the present day have the Holy Ghost, why are they so much at a loss to understand truth? Why do they walk in so many different ways and doctrines? Why do they need whole libraries of sermons, tracts, divinities, debates, arguments and opinions, all written by the wisdom of men, without even professing to be inspired? Well doth the Lord complain, saying, "their fear toward me is taught by the precept of men."

But to return, the apostles tarried at Jerusalem, until they were endowed with power, and then they commenced to proclaim the gospel. We have found that there is in the kingdom of God, first, a king crowned at the right hand of God, to whom is committed all power in heaven and on earth; second, commissioned officers, duly appointed to administer the affairs of government; third, the laws by which they were to be governed, which are ALL THINGS WHATSOEVER JESUS HAD COMMANDED HIS DISCIPLES TO TEACH THEM.

And now if we can find how men became citizens of that kingdom, in that age, should we not be dissatisfied with every thing in our age, which is represented to be the kingdom of God, and which is not according to the pattern?

There were no natural born subjects of the kingdom of God, except infants. Jesus said, "Suffer little children to come unto me and forbid them not, for of such is the kingdom of heaven." When they arrive to years of accountability they lose their citizenship in the kingdom, unless they are born of water and of the Spirit. Except infants, both Jews and Gentiles are included in sin and unbelief; and none can be citizens without the law of adoption, and all that believed on the name of the king, could be adopted: but there was but one invariable rule or plan by which they were adopted; and all that undertook to claim citizenship in any other way whatever, were counted thieves and robbers, and could never obtain the seal of adoption. This rule was laid down in the Savior's teaching to Nicodemus, namely:

"Except a man be born of water, [that is baptized in water], and of the Spirit, [that is baptized with the Spirit], he cannot enter into the kingdom of God."

Now to Peter, James and John, were given the keys of the kingdom, therefore it was their duty to open the kingdom to the Jews, and to the Gentiles. We will therefore carefully examine the manner in which Peter did adopt the Jews into the kingdom on the day of Pentecost.

Now when the multitude came running together on the day of Pentecost, the apostle Peter reasoned with them from the scriptures, testifying of Jesus Christ, and his resurrection and ascension on high, insomuch that many became convinced of the truth and enquired what they should do. These were not christians, but they were people who were then convinced that Jesus was the Christ, and because they were convinced of this fact, they inquired, "What shall we do?" Then Peter said unto them:

"Repent and be baptized, every one of you, in the name of Jesus Christ, for the remission of sins, and you shall receive the gift of the Holy Ghost; for the promise is unto you and your children, and to all that are afar off, even as many as the Lord our God shall call."

Reader, do you understand this proclamation? If you do you will see that this gospel is not generally preached in our day. Let us therefore analyze and examine it, sentence by sentence. You recollect they already believed, and the next thing was for them to repent: first, faith; second, repentance; third, baptism; fourth, remission of sins; and fifth, the Holy Ghost. This was the order of the gospel. Faith gave the power to become sons, or citizens; repentance and baptism in his name, for the remission of sins, was the obedience through which they were adopted; and the Holy Spirit of promise was the seal of their adoption, and this they were sure to receive after they obeyed. Now, reader, where do you hear such preaching in our day? Who teaches that those who believe and repent, should be baptized, and none others? Perhaps the reader may say the Baptists do; but do they call upon men to be baptized as soon as they believe and repent? And, moreover, do they promise the remission of sins, with the gift of the Holy Ghost? Recollect now, what effect the Holy Ghost has upon people who receive it. It will guide them into all truth, strengthen the memory, and show them things to come. And Joel has said it will cause them to dream dreams, to see visions, and to prophesy. O my reader, where do you find a gospel like this preached among men? Would men go mourning for weeks upon weeks, without the forgiveness of sins, or the comfort of the Holy Spirit, if Peter stood among us to tell us precisely how to get such blessings? Now what would you think of a camp-meeting, where three thousand men should come forward to be prayed for, and one of the ministers should (Peter like) command them every one to repent and be baptized for the remission of sins, promising that all who obeyed, should receive the remission of sins and the gift of the Holy Ghost, which should cause them to dream dreams and prophesy; and then should arise with his brethren of the same calling, and the same hour commence baptizing, and continue until they had baptized them all; and the Holy Ghost should fall upon them, and they begin to see visions, speak in other tongues and prophesy? Would not the news go abroad far and wide that a new doctrine had made its appearance, quite different from any thing now practiced among men? O yes, says the reader, this to be sure would be something new, and very strange to all of us. Well, strange as it may seem, it is the gospel which was preached by Peter on the day of Pentecost, and Paul declared that he preached the same gospel that Peter did, and he also said, "Though we, or an angel from heaven, preach any other gospel, let him be accursed." Now the reader need no longer be astonished to see that these signs do not follow them that believe another gospel, or doctrine, different from that preached by the apostles.

But now let us return to the kingdom of God organized in the days of the apostles. You discover that three thousand persons were adopted into the kingdom on the first day that the door was opened. These, together with the numerous additions which were afterwards made, were the subjects of this kingdom; which, being fitly framed together, grew unto an holy temple in the Lord. Thus we have cleared away the rubbish of sectarian tradition and superstition, which arose in heaps around us; and having searched carefully, we have at length discovered the kingdom of God, as it existed at its first organization, in the days of the apostles; and we have seen that it differs widely from all modern systems of religion, both in its offices, ordinances, powers, and privileges, insomuch that no man need ever mistake the one for the other.

Having made this discovery, we shall proceed to examine the progress of that kingdom among Jews and Gentiles; and what were its fruits, and what were the gifts and blessings which were enjoyed by its citizens.

Soon after the organization of the kingdom of God at Jerusalem, Philip came to Samaria, and there preached the gospel; and when they believed Philip, they were baptized, both men and women, and had great joy. And afterwards Peter and John came from Jerusalem, and prayed and laid their hands on them, and they received the Holy Ghost. Mark here, they first believed, and then were baptized, having great joy, and yet had not received the Holy Ghost. But that was given afterwards, by the laying on of hands and prayer, in the name of Jesus. O, how different from the systems of men!

Witness Paul's conversion while on his journey to Damascus. The Lord Jesus appeared to him in the way, but instead of telling him that his sins were forgiven, and pouring the Holy Ghost upon him, He sent him to Damascus, telling him that it should there be told him what he should do; and, coming to Damascus, Ananias being sent, commanded him not to tarry, but to "arise and be baptized and wash away his sins, calling on the name of the Lord." Then he arose and was baptized, and was even filled with the Holy Ghost, and straightway preached that Jesus was the Christ.

Witness Peter going to Cornelius, a Gentile of great piety, whose prayers were heard, and whose alms were remembered, and who had even attained to the ministering of an angel; yet with all his piety, and the Holy Ghost poured out upon him and his friends before they were baptized, they must be baptized, or they could not be saved. Why? Because the Lord had commanded the apostles to preach to every creature, and every creature who would not believe *and be baptized*, should be damned, without one exception. Witness the words of the angel to Cornelius: "He [Peter] shall tell you words, whereby thou and all thy house may be saved."

Query.—Could Cornelius have been saved without obeying the words of Peter? If so, the angel's errand was in vain.

Now, perhaps a minister who should find a man as good as Cornelius was, would say to him, Go on, brother, you can be saved, you have experienced religion, you may indeed be baptized to answer a good conscience, if you feel that it is your duty, or if not, it makes no difference, for a new heart is all that is really necessary to salvation. As much as to say that the commandments of Jesus are not absolutely necessary to salvation, and that a man may call him Lord, Lord, and be saved just as well as by keeping his commandments. O, vain and foolish doctrine! O, ye children of men, how have you perverted the gospel! In vain do you call him Lord, Lord, and do not obey his commandments.

Next we call to mind the jailer and his household, who were baptized in the same hour that they believed, without waiting for the light of day; and Lydia and her household, who attended to the ordinance the first sermon they heard on the subject; also Philip and the eunuch, who stopped the chariot at the first water they came to, in order to attend to the ordinance, and he had only heard of Jesus a few minutes before. Now, I gather from all those examples of ancient days, and from the precepts laid down in them, that baptism was the initiating ordinance by which all those who believed and repented were received and adopted into the church or kingdom of God, so as to be entitled to the remission of sins, and the blessings of the Holy Ghost. Indeed it was the ordinance through which they became sons and daughters; and because they were sons the Lord shed forth the Spirit of his Son into their hearts, crying Abba, Father. It is true that the Lord poured out the Holy Ghost upon Cornelius and his friends, before they were baptized, but it seemed necessary in order to convince the believing Jews that the Gentiles also had part in this salvation. After the apostles commenced to preach, I believe this is the only instance in the whole record, of people receiving the Holy Ghost without first obeying the laws of adoption. But mark! Obeying the laws of adoption would not constitute a man an heir of the kingdom—a citizen entitled to the gifts of the Spirit, unless these laws and ordinances were administered by one who had proper authority, and was duly commissioned from the king; and a commission given to one individual could never authorize another to act in his stead. This is one of the most important points, and it should be understood, for it brings to test every minister in Christendom; and shows the illegality of the organization of every church on earth, and all that have existed since direct inspiration ceased.

Now in order to understand this subject in plainness, let us examine the constitutions of earthly governments, in regard to the authority and laws of adoption. We will say for instance, the king or chief ruler of a nation, writes a commission to A. B., duly authorizing him to act in some office in the government; and, during his administration, two gentlemen from another nation come to reside in that nation, and, being strangers and foreigners, to become citizens, they go before A. B. and he administers the oath of allegiance in due form, and certifies the same, and this constitutes them legal citizens, entitled to all privileges of natural born citizens, or subjects.

After these things A. B. dies, and C. D. in looking over his papers happens to find the commission given to A. B., and, applying it to his own use, assumes the vacant office. Then two foreigners arrive and apply for citizenship, and being informed by persons ignorant of the affairs of government, that C. D. could administer the laws of adoption, they submit to be administered unto by C. D., without once examining his authority; C. D. certifies of their citizenship, and they suppose they have been legally adopted, the same as the others, and are entitled to all the privileges of citizenship, but by and by their citizenship is called in question, and they produce the certificate of C. D. The king or chief ruler inquires, "Who is C. D.? I never gave him a commission to act in any office, I know him not, and you are strangers and foreigners to the commonwealth, until you go before the legally appointed successor of A. B., or some other like authority who has a commission from me direct, in my own name." In the mean time, C. D. is taken and punished according to law for practicing imposition and usurping authority which was never conferred upon him. And so it is with the kingdom of God. The Lord authorized the Apostles and others by direct revelation, and by the spirit of prophecy, to preach and baptize, and build up his church and kingdom; but after awhile they died, and a long time passed away, and men reading over their commission, where it says to the eleven Apostles, "Go ye into all the world and preach the gospel to every creature," etc., they have had the presumption to apply these sayings as their authority, and without any other commission have gone forth professing to preach the gospel, and baptize, and build up the church and kingdom of God; but those whom they baptize, never receive the same blessings and gifts which characterized the Saints who were citizens of the kingdom in the days of the Apostles. Why? Because they are yet foreigners and strangers, for the commission given to the Apostles never commissioned any other man to act in their stead. This is a prerogative the Lord has reserved unto himself. No man has a right to take this ministry upon himself, but he that is called by revelation and duly qualified to act in his calling, by the Holy Ghost. But some may say with astonishment, "What? are none of all the ministers of the present day called to the ministry, and legally commissioned?"—Well, my reader, I will tell you how you may ascertain from their own mouths, and that will be far better than for me to answer. Go to the clergy, and ask them if God has given any direct revelation since the New Testament was finished; inquire of them whether the gift of prophecy ceased with the early age of the Church; and, in short, ask them if revelations, prophets, the ministering of angels, etc., are needed or expected in these days, or whether they believe that these things are done away no more to return to the earth? And their answer will be, that the Bible contains sufficient, and that since the canon of Scripture was filled revelation has ceased, the Spirit of prophecy has ceased, and the ministering of angels has ceased, because they are no longer needed. In short, they will denounce every man as an impostor who pretends to any such thing; and when you have obtained this answer, ask them how they, themselves, were called and commissioned to preach the gospel, and they will be at a loss to answer you, and will finally tell you the Bible commissioned them, saying, "Go ye into all the world," etc. Thus you see all who have no direct revelation from the king of heaven to themselves, neither by angels, nor the voice of God, nor by the Spirit of prophecy, are acting under authority which was given to others, who are dead, and their commission stolen, and their authority usurped, and the king may with propriety say, "I commissioned the eleven Apostles, but ye know me not, I never spoke to you; indeed, you believed it was not necessary for me to speak in your day; therefore you never sought in faith for any revelation, and I never gave you any, and even when I spake to others, you mocked them, and called them impostors, and persecuted them, because they testified of the things I had said unto them, therefore depart from me ye cursed, into everlasting fire prepared for the devil and his angels, for I was an hungered and ye fed me not, I was a stranger and ye took me not in, sick and in prison and ye visited me not." They may say, "Lord, when did we fail in any of these things?" The king will say, "Inasmuch as you have not done it unto the least of these, my brethren, (taking them for impostors, because they testified of the things which I have revealed unto them), ye have not done it unto me."

Having examined the kingdom of God, as to its offices and ordinances, and having discovered the only means of being adopted into it, let us examine more fully what are the blessings, privileges and enjoyments of its citizens. You have already seen that they were to cast out devils, speak with new tongues, heal the sick by the laying on of hands in the name of Jesus, as well as to see visions, dream dreams, prophesy, etc.

But let us look at the kingdom in its organized state, and see whether these promises were verified to Jews and Gentiles, wheresoever the kingdom of God was found in all ages of the world.

Paul wrote, first, "To the Church of God at Corinth;" second, "To them that are sanctified in Christ Jesus;" third, "To them that are called to be Saints;" and fourth, "To all that in every place call on the name of Jesus Christ our Lord." He said to them all, (*u*), "Now concerning spiritual *gifts*, brethren, I would not have you ignorant." And then continuing his instructions a few verses further on, he says:—

"But the manifestation of the Spirit is given to every man to profit withal. For to one is given by the Spirit the word of wisdom; to another, the word of knowledge by the same Spirit; to another, faith by the same Spirit; to another, the gift of healing by the same Spirit; to another, the working of miracles; to another, prophecy; to another, discerning of spirits; to another, divers kinds of tongues; to another, the interpretation of tongues; but all these worketh that one and the selfsame Spirit, dividing to every man severally as He [Christ] will. For as the body is one, and hath many members, and all the members of that one body, being many, are one body: so also is Christ. For by one Spirit are we all baptized into one body, whether we be Jews or Gentiles, whether we be bond or free; and have been all made to drink into one Spirit. For the body is not one member, but many. If the foot shall say because I am not the hand, I am not of the body; is it therefore not of the body? And if the ear shall say, because I am not the eye, I am not of the body, is it therefore not of the body? If the whole body were an eye, where were the smelling? But now hath God set

(*u*) 1 Cor. 12:1.

the members every one of them in the body, as it hath pleased him. And if they were all one member, where were the body?"

I reply, it would not exist.

"But now are they many members, yet but one body. And the eye cannot say unto the hand, I have no need of thee: nor again the head to the feet, I have no need of you. Nay, much more those members of the body which seem to be more feeble are necessary; and those members of the body which we think to be less honorable, upon these we bestow more abundant honor; and our uncomely parts have more abundant comeliness. For our comely parts have no need: but God hath tempered the body together, having given more abundant honor to that part which lacketh: that there should be no schism in the body; but that the members should have the same care one for another. And whether one member suffer, all the members suffer with it; or one member be honored, all the members rejoice with it. Now ye are the body of Christ, and members in particular. And God hath set some in the Church, first Apostles, secondarily Prophets, thirdly Teachers, after that miracles, then gifts of healing, helps, governments, diversities of tongues. Are all Apostles, are all Prophets, are all Teachers, are all workers of miracles, have all the gift of healing, do all speak with tongues, do all interpret. But covet earnestly the best gifts: and yet show I unto you a more excellent way."

From the thirteenth verse of the above chapter, we learn that the apostle is still speaking to the whole church in all ages, whether Jews or Gentiles, bond or free, even all who should ever compose the body of Christ, and showing that Christ's body consisted of many members, baptized by one Spirit into one body, possessing all these different gifts, some one gift and some another; and then he expressly says, that one member possessing one gift, should not say to another member, possessing another gift, we have no need of thee. And having shown that apostles, prophets, evangelists, pastors, and teachers; together with the gifts of prophecy, miracles, healing and all other gifts, compose the church, or body of Christ, in any age, both among Jews and Gentiles, bond and free; *and having utterly forbidden any of the members ever to say of any of these gifts, we have no need of thee;* he declares that the body never could be perfected without all of them, and that if they were done away there would be no body, that is, no church of Christ in existence. Having shown all these things, clearly, he exhorts them to covet earnestly the best gifts. And in the thirteenth chapter he exhorts them to have faith, hope, and charity, without which all these gifts would avail them nothing; and in the fourteenth chapter repeats the exhortation, "Follow after charity, and desire spiritual gifts; but rather that ye prophesy." In Ephesians, (*v*),

(*v*) Ephesians 1 : 17.

Paul prays that the Lord would give unto the church the Spirit of WISDOM and of REVELATION, in the KNOWLEDGE of God. In Ephesians, fourth chapter, he tells them that there is one body, and one Lord, one Spirit, one faith and one baptism, and that Christ ascended up on high, led captivity captive, and gave gifts to men, and he gave some apostles, and some prophets, and some evangelists, and some pastors and teachers, and if the reader inquires what these gifts or offices were for, let him read verse twelve where Paul says:

"For the perfecting of the Saints, for the work of the ministry, for the edifying of the body of Christ."

To show how long these were to continue, verse thirteen says:

"Till we all come in the unity of the faith, and of the knowledge of the Son of God, unto a perfect man, unto the measure of the stature of the fulness of Christ."

And if he still inquires what further object Christ had in giving these gifts, let him read verse fourteen:—

"That we henceforth be no more children, tossed to and fro, and carried about with every wind of doctrine, by the sleight of men, and cunning craftiness, whereby they lie in wait to deceive."

Now, without these gifts and offices, first, the Saints cannot be perfected; second, the work of the ministry cannot proceed; third, the body of Christ cannot be edified; and, fourth, there is nothing to prevent them from being carried about with every wind of doctrine. Now, I boldly declare that the reason for all the division, confusion, jars, discords and animosities; and the reason of so many faiths, lords, baptisms, and spirits; yea, the reason that their understanding is darkened, and that they are alienated from the life of God, through the ignorance that is in them, because of the blindness of their hearts; is all because they have no Apostles and Prophets, and other gifts, inspired from on high, to whom they give heed; for if they had such gifts and would give heed unto them, they would be built up in one body, in the pure doctrine of Christ, having one Lord, one faith, and one baptism, one hope of their calling; yea, they would be edified, built up unto Christ in all things, in whom the whole body fitly joined together, would grow into an holy temple in the Lord.

But so long as men, by their cunning craftiness, can persuade them that they have no need of these things, so long they can toss them about, with every wind of doctrine just as they please.

Now reader, I have concluded my examination of the kingdom of God, as it existed in the Apostles' days; and we cannot look at it in any subsequent age, until it was renewed again in the last days, for it never did, and never will exist, without Apostles and Prophets, and all the other gifts of the Spirit.

Were we to take a view of the churches, from the days that inspiration ceased until now, we should see nothing like the kingdom which we have been viewing with such admiration and delight. But instead of Apostles and Prophets, we would see false teachers whom men had heaped to themselves, and instead of the gifts of the Spirit, we should see the wisdom of men; and instead of the Holy Ghost, many false spirits; instead of the ordinances of God, commandments of men; instead of knowledge, opinion; guess work, instead of revelation; division, instead of union; doubt, instead of faith; despair, instead of hope; hatred, instead of charity; a physician, instead of the laying on of hands for the healing of the sick; fables, instead of truth; evil, instead of good; darkness, instead of light; and, in a word, anti-Christ, instead of Christ; the powers of earth having made war with the Saints, and overcome them, until the words of God should be fulfilled. O, my God, shut up the vision! for my heart sickens while I gaze; and let the day hasten on when the earth shall be cleansed by fire from such awful pollutions; but, first, let thy promise be fulfilled, which thou didst make by the mouth of thy prophet Jeremiah, concerning "Thy people, the remnant of Israel," saying,

"Behold, I will bring them from the north country, and gather them from the coasts of the earth. * * * They shall come and sing in the height of Zion, and shall flow together to the goodness of the Lord, for wheat, and for wine, and for oil, and for the young of the flock and the herd; and their soul shall be as a watered garden; and they shall not sorrow any more at all." (*w*)

(*w*) Jeremiah 31 : 8-12.

## CHAPTER IV.

### BOOK OF MORMON—ORIGIN OF THE AMERICAN INDIANS, ETC.

Ye gloomy scenes! far hence, intrude no more!
Sublimer themes, invite the muse to soar
In loftier strains, while scenes both strange and new,
Burst on the sight, and open to the view.

Lo! from the opening heavens in bright array,
An angel comes—to earth he bends his way!
Reveals to man, in power, as at the first,
The fulness of the gospel long since lost.

See earth obedient, from its bosom yield,
The sacred truth it faithfully concealed;
The wise confounded, startled at the sight;
The proud and haughty tremble with affright.

The hireling priests against the truth engage,
While hell beneath, stands trembling, filled with rage;
False are their hopes, and all their struggles vain;
Their craft must fall, and with it all their gain;
The deaf must hear, the meek their joy increase;
The poor be glad, and their oppressions cease.

While darkness covered the earth and gross darkness the people, every man walking in his own way, and looking for his gain from his quarter; the Lord having for a long time holden his peace, and the people fondly flattering themselves that the voice of inspiration would never again sound in the ears of mortals, to disturb or molest them in their sinful career; while a few were looking for the consolation of Israel, and crying to God for the ushering in of that long expected day, when an angel should fly through the midst of heaven, having the everlasting gospel to preach unto them that dwell on the earth, suddenly a voice was heard, a cry saluted the ears of mortals, a testimony was heard among them, piercing to the inmost recesses of their hearts, when all at once the heathen began to rage, and the people to imagine a vain thing;

the clergy lifted a warning voice, crying, "Impostor, false prophets, beware of delusion, etc.;" while the professor of religion, the drunkard, the swearer, the learned and the ignorant, soon caught the sound and reiterated it again and again. Thus it re-echoed from one end of our country to the other for a long time, and when any one was so fortunate as to retain his sober senses and candidly inquire, "What is the matter?" the reply was, "We hardly know anything about it; but suffice it to say, some fellows have made their appearance, Paul like, who testify something about the ministering of angels, or some revelation or inspiration; just as though the religion of ancient days, and the faith once delivered to the Saints, were returning to the earth in this enlightened age; so that not only this our craft is in danger, but our modern systems of religion, built upon the wisdom and learning of men without direct inspiration, are likely to be spoken against, and their great magnificence despised, which all the world worships." And then all again cry with a loud voice, saying, "Great is the wisdom of man, great are the systems of modern divinity, great is the wisdom of uninspired priests who come to us with excellency of speech, and with man's wisdom determined to know nothing among us, save the opinions and creeds of their own, and their speech and their preaching is with enticing words of man's wisdom, not in demonstration of the Spirit, and of power, for that is done away, that our faith should not stand in the power of God, but in the wisdom of men."

In the midst of the noise and clamor, and prejudice of an opposing world, it is difficult to get the people to understand the facts in the case in relation to one of the most important subjects ever presented to the consideration of mankind.

The Book of Mormon has perhaps been less understood and more misrepresented, by the world at large, than any other publication which ever appeared. America and England have, as it were, been flooded with publications against the said book, and many of them were written by those who had never seen the book, or by those who had only read one or two pages in it, or slightly looked through it, with a biased mind and a determination to find fault. By some of these it has been represented as a romance. By others as a new Bible, calculated to displace or do away with the Bible. Some have pronounced it as a "silly mess of stuff," not worth the perusal; and others as the most ingenious literary work ever put together. Some have found fault with it for being so much like the Bible, and agreeing with it; and others have condemned it as being not enough like the Bible, and disagreeing with it. Some have denounced it as notoriously corrupt, immoral, and blasphemous in its principles; and others have condemned it for being so exceedingly pure and moral in its principles as to be just calculated to deceive. One clergyman in particular, in a tract of sixty pages on this book, condemns it for being "a strange mixture of *faith* and *works*, of the *mercy* of God and obedience of the *creature*." Some literary persons have pronounced it as altogether *ancient* in its *style, language*, and *subjects*, and as bearing great internal evidence of its own antiquity; while others have condemned it as bearing every mark of being a *modern* production. Some have said that there were no definite predictions of the future contained in it, by the fulfillment or failure of which its prophetic merits might be tested; and others have quoted largely from its most plain and pointed predictions which relate to circumstances about to be fulfilled, and have condemned it on account of its plainness.

In the midst of all these jarring statements, it is our duty to show, as far as possible, what the Book of Mormon really is.

When the Lord confounded the languages of Babel he led forth a colony from thence to the western continent, which is now called America. This colony, after crossing the ocean in eight vessels, and landing in this country, became in process of time a great nation. They inhabited America for some fifteen hundred years. They were at length destroyed, for their wickedness, about six hundred years before Christ. A prophet by the name of Ether wrote their history, and an account of their destruction. Ether lived to witness their entire destruction, and deposited his record where it was afterwards found by a colony of Israelites who came from Jerusalem, six hundred years before Christ, and who re-peopled America. This last colony were descendants of the tribe of Joseph. They grew and multiplied, and finally became two mighty nations. One of these nations was called Nephites, Nephi being their founder; the other was called Lamanites, after a leader by the name of Laman. The Lamanites became a dark and benighted people, of whom the American Indians are still a remnant. The Nephites were a civilized and enlightened people, and a people highly favored of the Lord, who had visions, angels, and the gift of prophecy among them from age to age, and finally, they were blessed with the personal appearance of

Jesus Christ after His resurrection; from whose mouth they received the doctrine of the gospel, and a knowledge of the future, down through all succeeding ages. But after all the blessings and privileges were conferred upon them, they fell into great wickedness in the third and fourth centuries of the Christian era, and finally were destroyed by the hands of the Lamanites. This destruction took place about A. D. 420.

Mormon, by the commandment of the Lord, made an abridgment of the sacred records, which contained the history of his forefathers, and the prophecies and gospel which had been revealed among them; to which he added a sketch of the history of his own time, and the destruction of his nation. Previous to his death the abridged records fell into the hands of his son, Moroni, who continued them down to A. D. 420, at which time he deposited them carefully in the earth, on a hill which was then called Cumorah, which was situated in Ontario Co., township of Manchester, and State of New York, North America. This he did in order to preserve them from the Lamanites, who overrun the country and sought to destroy them and all the records pertaining to the Nephites. This record has lain concealed, or sealed up, from A. D. 420, to September 22nd, 1827; at which time it was found by Mr. Joseph Smith, jun., he being directed by an angel of the Lord to go and obtain it.

The following account of the discovery and translation of this record is extracted from a tract by Elder Orson Pratt, published at Edinburgh, 1840, entitled, "Remarkable Visions," etc., to which our readers are referred for further particulars:—

"How far below the surface these records were [anciently] placed, I am unable to say; but from the fact, that they had been some fourteen hundred years buried, and that, too, on the side of a hill so steep, one is ready to conclude, that they were some feet below, as the earth would naturally wear, more or less, in that length of time. But they, being placed toward the top of the hill, the ground would not remove as much as at two thirds, perhaps. Another circumstance would prevent the wearing of the earth; in all probability, as soon as timber had time to grow, the hill was covered, and the roots of the same would hold the surface. However, on this point, I shall leave every man to draw his own conclusion, and form his own speculation. But, suffice to say, a hole of sufficient depth was dug. At the bottom of this was laid a stone of suitable size, the upper surface being smooth. At each edge was placed a large quantity of cement, and into this cement, at the four edges of this stone, were placed erect four others; *their* bottom edges resting in the cement, at the outer edges of the first stone. The four last named, when placed erect, formed a box: the corners, or where the edges of the four came in contact, were also cemented so firmly that the moisture from without was prevented from entering. It is to be observed, also, that the inner surfaces of the four erect or side stones, were smooth. This box was sufficiently large to admit a breastplate, such as was used by the ancients to defend the chest, etc., from the arrows and weapons of their enemy. From the bottom of the box, or from the breastplate, arose three small pillars, composed of the same description of cement used on the edges; and upon these three pillars were placed the records. This box containing the records, was covered with another stone, the bottom surface being flat, and the upper crowning. When it was first visited by Mr. Smith, on the morning of the 22nd of September, 1823, a part of the crowning stone was visible above the surface, while the edges were concealed by the soil and grass. From which circumstance, it may be seen, that however deep this box might have been placed at first, the time had been sufficient to wear the earth, so that it was easily discovered, when once directed, and yet not enough to make a perceivable difference to the passer by. After arriving at the repository, a little exertion in removing the soil from the edges of the top of the box, and a light pry, brought to his natural vision its contents. While viewing and contemplating this sacred treasure with wonder and astonishment, behold! the angel of the Lord, who had previously visited him, again stood in his presence, and his soul was again enlightened as it was the evening before, and he was filled with the Holy Spirit, and the heavens were opened, and the glory of the Lord shone round about and rested upon him. While he thus stood gazing and admiring, the angel said, 'Look!' And as he thus spake, he beheld the Prince of Darkness, surrounded by his innumerable train of associates. All this passed before him, and the heavenly messenger said, 'All this is shown, the good and evil, the holy and the impure, the glory of God and the power of darkness, that you may know hereafter the two powers, and never be influenced or overcome by that wicked one. Behold, whatsoever enticeth and leadeth to good, and to do good, is of God, and whatsoever doth not, is of that wicked one. It is he that filleth the hearts of men with evil, to walk in darkness and blaspheme God; and you may learn from henceforth, that his ways are to destruction, but the way of holiness is peace and rest. You cannot at this time obtain this record, for the commandment of God is strict, and if ever these sacred things are obtained, they must be by prayer and faithfulness in obeying the Lord. They are not deposited here for the sake of accumulating gain and wealth for the glory of this world; they were sealed by the prayer of faith, and because of the knowledge which they contain, they are of no worth among the children of men, only for their knowledge. On them is contained the fulness of the gospel of Jesus Christ, as it was given to His people on this land; and when it shall be brought forth by the power of God, it shall be carried to the Gentiles, of whom many will receive it, and after will the seed of Israel be brought into the fold of their Redeemer by obeying it also. Those who kept the commandments of the Lord on this land, desired this at his hand, and through the prayer of faith obtained the promise, that if their descendants should transgress and fall away, a record should be kept, and in the last days come to their children. These things are sacred, and must be kept so, for the promise of the Lord concerning them must be fulfilled. No man can obtain them if his heart is impure, because they contain that which is sacred. * * *

By them will the Lord work a great and marvelous work; the wisdom of the wise shall become as nought, and the understanding of the prudent shall be hid, and because the power of God shall be displayed, those who profess to know the truth, but walk in deceit, shall tremble with anger: but with signs and with wonders, with gifts and with healings, with the manifestations of the power of God, and with the Holy Ghost, shall the hearts of the faithful be comforted. You have now beheld the power of God manifested, and the power of Satan; you see that there is nothing desirable in the works of darkness; that they cannot bring happiness; that those who are overcome therewith are miserable; while, on the other hand, the righteous are blessed with a place in the kingdom of God, where joy unspeakable surrounds them. There they rest beyond the power of the enemy of truth, where no evil can disturb them. The glory of God crowns them, and they continually feast upon His goodness, and enjoy His smiles. Behold, notwithstanding you have seen this great display of power, by which you may ever be able to detect the evil one, yet I give unto you another sign, and when it comes to pass, then know that the Lord is God, and that He will fulfill His purposes, and that the knowledge which this record contains, will go to every nation, and kindred, and tongue, and people under the whole heaven. This is the sign: when these things begin to be known, that is when it is known that the Lord has shown you these things, the workers of iniquity will seek your overthrow. They will circulate falsehoods to destroy your reputation; and also will seek to take your life; but remember this, if you are faithful, and shall hereafter continue to keep the commandments of the Lord, you shall be preserved to bring these things forth; for in due time He will give you a commandment to come and take them. When they are interpreted, the Lord will give the holy priesthood to some, and they shall begin to proclaim this gospel and baptize by water, and after that, they shall have power to give the Holy Ghost by the laying on of hands. Then will persecution rage more and more; for the iniquities of men shall be revealed, and those who are not built upon the Rock will seek to overthrow the church; but it will increase the more opposed, and spread farther and farther, increasing in knowledge till they shall be sanctified, and receive an inheritance where the glory of God will rest upon them; and when this takes place, and all things are prepared, the ten tribes of Israel will be revealed in the north country, whither they have been for a long season; and when this is fulfilled will be brought to pass that saying of the prophet, 'And the Redeemer shall come to Zion, and unto them that turn from transgression in Jacob, saith the Lord.' But, notwithstanding the workers of iniquity shall seek your destruction, the arm of the Lord will be extended, and you will be borne off conqueror, if you keep all His commandments. Your name shall be known among the nations; for the work which the Lord will perform by your hands shall cause the righteous to rejoice and the wicked to rage; with the one it shall be had in honor, and with the other in reproach; yet with these it shall be a terror, because of the great and marvelous work which shall follow the coming forth of this fulness of the gospel. Now go thy way, remembering what the Lord has done for thee, and be diligent in keeping His commandments, and He will deliver thee from temptations, and from all the arts and devices of the wicked one. Forget not to pray, that thy mind may become strong, that when He shall manifest unto thee thou mayest have power to escape the evil, and to obtain these precious things.'"

We here remark that the above quotation is partly an extract from a letter written by Elder Oliver Cowdery, which was published in one of the numbers of the *Latter Day Saints' Messenger and Advocate.*

Although many more instructions were given by the mouth of the angel to Mr. Smith which we do not write in this book, yet the most important items are contained in the foregoing relation. During the period of the four following years, he frequently received instruction from the mouth of the heavenly messenger; and on the morning of the 22nd of September, A. D. 1827, the angel of the Lord delivered the records into his hands.

These records were engraved on plates, which had the appearance of gold. Each plate was not far from seven by eight inches in width and length, being not quite as thick as common tin. They were filled on both sides with engravings, in Reformed Egyptian characters, and bound together in a volume as the leaves of a book, and fastened at the edge with three rings running through the whole. This volume was something near six inches in thickness, a part of which was sealed. The characters or letters upon the unsealed part were small, and beautifully engraved. The whole book exhibited many marks of antiquity in its construction, as well as much skill in the art of engraving. With the records was found a curious instrument, called by the ancients the Urim and Thummim, which consisted of two transparent stones, clear as crystal, set in two rims of a bow. This was in use in ancient times by persons called seers. It was an instrument by the use of which they received revelation of things distant, or of things past or future.

In the meantime, the inhabitants of that vicinity having been informed that Mr. Smith had seen heavenly visions, and that he had discovered sacred records, began to ridicule and mock. And after he had obtained these sacred things, while proceeding home through the wilderness and fields, he was waylaid by two ruffians, who had secreted themselves for the purpose of robbing him of the records. One of them struck him with a club before he perceived them; but, being a strong man and large in stature, with great exertion he cleared himself from them and ran towards home, being closely pursued until he came near his father's house, when his pursuers, for fear of being detected, turned and fled the other way.

Soon the news of his discoveries spread abroad throughout all those parts. False reports, misrepresentations, and base slanders, flew as if upon the wings of the wind in every direction. The house was frequently beset by mobs and evil designing persons. Several times he was shot at, and very narrowly escaped. Every device was used to get the plates away from him. And, being continually in danger of losing his life, he at length concluded to leave the place and go to Pennsylvania; and accordingly he packed up his goods, putting the plates into a barrel of beans, and proceeded upon his journey. He had not gone far before he was overtaken by an officer with a search warrant, who flattered himself with the idea that he should surely obtain the plates; after searching very diligently he was sadly disappointed at not finding them. Mr. Smith then drove on; but, before he got to his journey's end, he was again overtaken by an officer on the same business, who, after ransacking the wagon very carefully, went his way, as much chagrined as the first at not being able to discover the object of his search. Without any further molestation he pursued his journey until he came into the northern part of Pennsylvania, near the Susquehanna river, where his father-in-law resided.

Having provided himself with a home he commenced translating the record, by the gift and power of God through the means of the Urim and Thummim; and, being a poor writer, he was under the necessity of employing a scribe to write the translation as it came from his mouth.

In the mean time a few of the original characters were accurately transcribed and translated by Mr. Smith, which, with the translation, were taken by a gentleman by the name of Martin Harris to the city of New York, where they were presented to a learned gentleman by the name of Anthon, who professed to be extensively acquainted with many languages, both ancient and modern.

"Professor Anthon said that the translation was correct, more so than any he had before seen translated from the Egyptian. I then showed him those which were not yet translated, and he said that they were Egyptian, Chaldaic, Assyriac, and Arabic, and he said that they were the true characters. He gave me a certificate certifying to the people of Palmyra that they were true characters, and that the translation of such of them as had been translated was also correct. I took the certificate and put it into my pocket, and was just leaving the house when Mr. Anthon called me back and asked me how the young man found out that there were gold plates in the place where he found them. I answered that an angel of God had revealed it unto him. He then said to me, 'Let me see that certificate.' I accordingly took it out of my pocket and gave it to him, when he took it and tore it to pieces, saying that there was no such thing now as ministering of angels, and that if I would bring the plates to him he would translate them. I informed him that part of the plates were sealed, and that I was forbidden to bring them. He replied, 'I cannot read a sealed book.' I left him and went to Dr. Mitchell, who sanctioned what Professor Anthon had said, respecting both the characters and the translation." (*x*)

Mr. Smith continued the work of translation, as his pecuniary circumstances would permit, until he finished the unsealed part of the records. The part translated is entitled the "Book of Mormon," which contains nearly as much reading as the Old Testament.

"Well," says the objector, "If it were not for the marvelous, the book would be considered one of the greatest discoveries which the world ever witnessed." Had Mr. Smith been ploughing, or digging a well or cellar, and accidentally dug up a record containing some account of the ancient history of this continent, and its original inhabitants, together with the origin of the Indian tribes who now inhabit it; had this record nothing to do with God or angels or inspiration, it would have been hailed by all the learned of America and Europe as one of the greatest and most important discoveries of modern time, one which unfolded a mystery that has bid defiance to all the researches of the learned world. Every newspaper would have been filled with the glad tidings, while its contents would have poured in upon the world a flood of light on subjects before concealed in the labyrinth of uncertainty and doubt. It is repugnant to the people of this age, who boast of their enlightenment, religion and wisdom, to acknowledge that there is any necessity for the ministering of angels, or for inspiration. They say, "This is too much; away with such things, for they come in contact with the wisdom and popularity of this enlightened age." The Lord knew what they would say in reference to this work, and it has come forth just as the prophets foretold that it would. The Lord always takes a different course from that which is marked out for Him by the wisdom of the world, so that he may confound the wise and bring to nought the understanding of the prudent. He chooses men of low degree, even the simple and the unlearned, and those who are despised, to do his work and to bring about

(*x*) Times and Sersons, vol. 3, page 773.

his purposes, that no flesh shall glory in his presence. O ye wise, and ye learned, who despise the wisdom that comes from above! know ye not that it is impossible for the world by wisdom to find out God? know ye not that all your wisdom is foolishness with God? know ye not that ye must become as little children, and be willing to learn wisdom from the least of his servants, or you will perish in your ignorance?

But what are the evidences which we gather from Scripture concerning the coming forth of this glorious work? We shall attempt to prove: first, that America is a promised land to the seed of Joseph; second, that the Lord promised to reveal to them His truth as well as to the Jews; and third, that their record was to come forth and be united with the record of the Jews in time for the restoration of Israel in the last days.

First, Jacob, while blessing the two sons of Joseph, says.

"Let them grow into a multitude in the midst of the earth." (y)

In the same blessing it is said of Ephraim, his seed shall become a multitude of nations. Now put the sense of these sayings together, and it shows that Ephraim was to be a multitude of nations in the midst of the earth. In Genesis (z) it was prophesied concerning Joseph, (in Jacob's blessing), that he should be "a fruitful bough by a well, whose branches run over the wall; the archers have sorely grieved him and shot at him, and hated him, yet his bow abode in strength." Again, he further says:—

"The blessings of thy father have prevailed above the blessings of my progenitors, unto the utmost bound of the everlasting hills; they shall be on the head of Joseph, and on the crown of the head of him that was separate from his brethren."

Now, I ask, who were Jacob's progenitors, and what was the blessing they conferred upon him? Abraham and Isaac were his progenitors, and the land of Canaan was the blessing that they conferred upon him, or that God promised that he should possess. Recollect that Jacob conferred on Joseph a much greater land than that of Canaan; even greater than his fathers had conferred upon him, for Joseph's blessing was to extend to the utmost bound of the everlasting hills. Now reader, stand in Egypt, where Jacob then stood, and go to the utmost bound of the everlasting hills, and you will land somewhere in the central part of America. Again, one of the prophets says, in speaking of Ephraim, "When the Lord shall roar, the children of Ephraim shall tremble from the west."

(y) Gen 48:16, (z) Gen. 49:22.

Now let us sum up these sayings, and what have we gained? First, that Ephraim was to grow into a multitude of nations in the midst of the earth; second, that Joseph was to be greatly blessed in a large inheritance, as far off as America; third, that this was to be on the west of Egypt or Jerusalem.

Now let the world search from pole to pole, and they will not find a multitude of nations in the midst of the earth, who can possibly have sprung from Ephraim, unless they can find them in America; for the other parts of the earth are inhabited by mixed races, who have sprung from various sources; while here an almost boundless country was secluded from the rest of the world, and inhabited by a race of men, evidently of the same origin, although as evidently divided into many nations. Now the Scriptures cannot be broken, therefore, these Scriptures must apply to America, for the plainest of reasons—because they can apply no where else. Secondly, God revealed himself to the seed of Joseph or Ephraim, dwelling in America. Speaking of Ephraim, he says, by the spirit of prophecy,—

"I have written unto him the great things of my law, but they were counted as a strange thing." (a)

This is proof positive, and needs no comment, that the great truths of heaven were revealed unto Ephraim, and were counted as a strange thing.

Third, these writings were to come forth just previous to the gathering of Israel. The word of the Lord came unto Ezekiel, saying:—

"Moreover, thou son of man, take thee one stick, and write upon it, 'For Judah, and for the children of Israel, his companions:' then take another stick and write upon it, 'For Joseph, the stick of Ephraim, and for all the house of Israel, his companions:' and join them one to another into one stick; and they shall become one in thine hand. And when the children of thy people shall speak unto thee, saying, 'Wilt thou not shew us what thou meanest by these?' Say unto them, 'Thus saith the Lord God; behold, I will take the stick of Joseph, which is in the hand of Ephraim, and the tribes of Israel his fellows, and will put them with him, even with the stick of Judah, and make them one stick, and they shall be one in mine hand. And the sticks whereon thou writest shall be in thine hand before their eyes.' And say unto them; thus saith the Lord God: 'Behold I will take the children of Israel from among the heathen, whither they be gone, and will gather them on every side, and bring them into their own land: and I will make them one nation in the land upon the mountains of Israel; and one king shall be king to them all: and they shall be no more two nations, neither shall they be divided into two kingdoms any more at all: neither shall they defile themselves

(a) Hosea 8 : 12.

any more with their idols, nor with their detestable things, nor with any of their transgressions: but I will save them out of all their dwelling-places, wherein they have sinned, and will cleanse them: so shall they be my people, and I will be their God."

Two writings are presented; one to Ephraim, and one to Judah; that of Ephraim was to be brought forth by the Lord and put with that of Judah, and they were to become one in their testimony, and were to grow together in this manner, in order to bring about the gathering of Israel. The eighty-fifth Psalm is very plain on the subject; speaking of the restoration of Israel to their own land it says,—

"Mercy and truth are met together; righteousness and peace have kissed each other. *Truth shall spring out of the earth*, and righteousness shall look down from heaven. Yea, the Lord shall give that which is good, and our land shall yield her increase. Righteousness shall go before him, and shall set us in the way of his steps."

Now the Savior while praying for his disciples, said, "Sanctify them through thy *truth*, thy *word* is *truth*." From these passages we learn that His word was to spring out of the earth, while righteousness was to look down from heaven. Then Israel was to be set in the way of His steps, and partake of the fruit of their own land. The Lord, by Jeremiah, said,—

"I will bring it [Jerusalem] health and cure, and will cure them *and will reveal unto them the abundance of peace and truth*. And I will cause the captivity of Israel and the captivity of Judah to return, and will build them as at the first." (*b*)

And Isaiah, speaking of the everlasting covenant which should gather them, makes this extraordinary and very remarkable expression: "Their seed shall be known among the Gentiles, and their offspring among the people." The Indians of America are of Israel, as some of their manners, customs and traditions indicate, and they are now to a great extent "among the Gentiles," especially in Mexico, Central and South America.

So much then we have produced from the Scriptures in proof of a work like the Book of Mormon making its appearance in these days; to say nothing of Isaiah twenty-ninth.

[We now refer the reader to the Analysis of Isaiah 29th chapter, to be found at the end of this book].

"But," says one, "what is the use of the Book of Mormon, even if it be true?" I answer, first, it brings to light an important history, before unknown to man. Second, it reveals

(*b*) Jer. 33 : 6, 7,

the origin of the American Indians, which was before a mystery. Third, it contains important prophecies, yet to be fulfilled, which immediately concern the present generation. Fourth, it contains much plainness in regard to points of doctrine, insomuch that all my understand, and see eye to eye, if they take pains to read it. But what are its proofs, as to chosen witnesses who testify to its translation by inspiration? For this testimony I refer the reader to the testimony of the witnesses in the first part of the Book of Mormon. He will there find as positive testimony as has ever been found in the other Scriptures, concerning any truth which God ever revealed. Men there testify, not only that they have seen and handled the plates, but that an angel of God came down from heaven, and presented the plates before them, while the glory of God shone round them; and the voice of God spoke from heaven, and told them that these things were true, and had been translated by the gift and power of God, and commanded them to bear record of the same to all people. Blessed be the Lord God of our fathers, he has visited his people, and the dayspring from on high has dawned upon our benighted world once more; for no sooner had the book been translated, and men begun to bear record of the same, than the angel of the Lord came down from heaven again, and commissioned men to preach the gospel to every creature, and to baptize with water for the remission of sins. No sooner did the people begin to believe their testimony and be baptized, than the Holy Ghost fell on them through the laying on of hands in the name of Jesus; and the heavens were opened, and while some had the ministering of angels, others began to speak in other tongues, and prophesy. From that time forth many of them were healed by the laying on of hands, in the name of Jesus; and thus mightily grew the word of God, and prevailed; and thousands have been raised up to testify that they do know for themselves, and are not dependent on the testimony of any man for the truth of these things, for these signs follow them that believe; and when a man believes the truth through the testimony of God's witnesses, and when these signs follow not only them, but himself also, if he has the ministering of angels, if he has been healed, or heals others by the laying on of hands in Jesus' name, or if he speaks in other tongues, or prophesies, he knows it for himself; and thus is fulfilled the saying of the Scripture, "If any man will do His will he shall know of the doctrine whether it be of God." Thus faith comes by hearing, and knowledge by obeying; and hearing comes by preaching, and preaching comes by sending; as it is written,—"How shall they preach except they be sent?"

There are many who say, "Show us a sign and we will believe." Remember that faith comes not by signs; but signs come by faith, and gifts were not given to make people believe; for what saith the Scripture? "Gifts are for the edifying of the Church." If otherwise why was it not written that faith comes by miracles? But it is written, "Faith comes by hearing." I always take it for granted that a man or woman who demands a sign in order to make them believe, belongs to a wicked and adulterous generation at least to say no worse; for any person who will go to Jesus, with a pure heart, desiring and praying in faith that they may know the truth concerning these things, the Lord will reveal it to them, and they shall know, and shall bear testimony; for by the Spirit of God, they shall know truth from error; as it is written, "My sheep hear my voice." And he that will not come to Jesus in faith, shall never know the truth until he shall find that the harvest is over, and the summer is ended, and his soul is not saved.

Thus the religion of Jesus, unlike all other religious systems, bears its own weight and brings certainty and knowledge, leaving no room for imposition. And now I say again unto all people, Come unto the Father in the name of Jesus; doubt not, but be believing, as in days of old, and ask in faith for whatsoever you stand in need, ask not that you may consume it on your lusts; but ask with a firmness not to be shaken. Yield to no temptation, but keep his commandments, as far as he makes them manifest unto you, and if you do this, and he reveals to you that he has sent us with a new and everlasting covenant and commanded us to preach, and to baptize, and to build up his Church, as in days of old, then come forward and obey the truth; but if you do not know, or are not satisfied that He has sent us, then do not embrace the doctrine we preach. Thus to your own master you shall stand or fall; and one day you shall know; yea, in that great day, when every knee shall bow, then shall you know that God has sent us with the truth to prune his vineyard for the last time with a mighty pruning.

We offer circumstantial evidence from "American Antiquities," and from the traditions of the natives, etc.

Mr. Boudinot says:—

"It is said among their principal or beloved men, that they have it handed down from their ancestors that such a book as the white people have was once theirs; that while they had it they prospered exceedingly, etc. They also say that their fathers were possessed of an extraordinary Divine Spirit, by which they foretold future events, and controlled the common course of nature; and this they transmitted to their offspring, on condition of their obeying the sacred laws; that they did by these means bring down showers of blessings upon their beloved people; but that this power for a long time past has entirely ceased."

Col. James Smith, in his journal, while a prisoner among the natives, says:—

"They have a tradition, that in the beginning of this continent, the angels, or heavenly inhabitants, as they call them, frequently visited the people, and talked with their forefathers, and gave directions how to pray."

Mr. Boudinot, in his able work remarks concerning their language:—

"Their language in its roots, idiom, and particular construction, appears to have the whole genius of the Hebrew; and, what is very remarkable, and well worthy of serious attention, has most of the peculiarities of the language, especially those in which it differs from most other languages. There is a tradition related by an aged Indian of the Stockbridge tribe, that their fathers were once in possession of a 'Sacred Book' which was *handed down from generation to generation and at last hid in the earth*, since which time they had been under the feet of their enemies. But those oracles were to be restored to them again, and then they would triumph over their enemies and regain their ancient country, together with their rights and priviliges." Mr. Boudinot, after recording many traditions similar to the above, at length remarks: "Can any man read this short account of Indian traditions, drawn from the tribes of various nations, from the west to the east, and from the south to the north, wholly separated from each other, written by different authors of the best character, both for knowledge and integrity, possessing the best means of information, at various and distant times, without any possible communication with each other, and yet suppose that all this is the effect of chance, accident or design, from a love of the marvelous, or premeditated intention of deceiving, and thereby ruining their well established reputation?"

Joseph Merrick, Esq., a highly respected character in Pittsfield, Mass., gave the following account:—

"That in 1815, he was leveling some ground under and near an old woodshed standing on a place of his, situated on Indian Hill. He ploughed and conveyed away old chips and earth, to some depth. After the work was done, walking over the place, he discovered, near where the earth had been dug the deepest, a black strap, as it appeared, about six inches in length, and one and a half in breadth, and about the thickness of a leather trace to a harness. He perceived it had at each end a loop of some hard substance. probably for the purpose of carrying it. He conveyed it to his house and threw it into an old tool box. He afterwards found it thrown out at the door, and again conveyed it to the box.

After some time, he thought he would examine it, but in attempting to cut it, found it as hard as bone; he succeeded however in getting it open, and found it was formed of two pieces of thick rawhide, sewed and made water tight with the sinews of some animal, and gummed over; and in the fold was contained *four folded pieces of parchment.* They were of a dark yellow hue, and contained some kind of writing. The neighbors, coming in to see the strange discovery, tore one of the pieces to atoms, in the true Hun and Vandal style. The other three pieces Mr. Merrick saved, and sent them to Cambridge, where they were examined, and discovered to have been written with a pen, in *Hebrew*, plain and legible. The writing on the three remaining pieces of parchment was quotations from the Old Testament. See Deut. c. 6, from 4th to 9th v. inclusive; also, c. 11, v. 13 to 21, inclusive, and Exodus, c. 13, v. 11 to 16, inclusive, to which the reader can refer, if he has the curiosity to read this most interesting discovery."

"On the banks of White River, in Arkansas Territory, have been found the remains of an enlightened population of the most extraordinary character, on account of their dimensions and the materials of which they were erected. One of these works is a wall of earth, which encloses an area of six hundred and forty acres, equal to a mile square, and having in its centre the foundation of a large circular building, or temple. Another, yet more strange and more extended, consists of the foundations of a great city, whose streets, crossing each other at right angles, are easily traced through the mighty forest. And besides them are found the foundations of *houses*, made of *burned bricks* like the bricks of the present time. These have been traced to the extent of a mile."

The foregoing is taken from *Priest's American Antiquities*, and from the same work we extract the following, page 216.

"*Ruins of the City of Otolum, discovered in North America.*—In a letter of C. S. Rafinesque, whom we have before quoted, to a correspondent in Europe, we find the following: 'Some years ago the Society of Geography, in Paris, offered a large premium for a voyage to Guatamala, and for a new survey of the antiquities of Yucatan and Chiapa, chiefly those fifteen miles from Palenque.'

"'I have,' says this author, 'restored to them the true name of *Otolum*, which is yet the name of the stream running through the ruins. They were surveyed by Captain Del Rio, in 1787, an account of which was published in English in 1822. This account describes partly the ruins of a *stone* city, of no less dimensions than seventy-five miles in circuit; length thirty-two, and breadth twelve miles, full of palaces, monuments, statues, and inscriptions; one of the earliest seats of American civilization, about equal to Thebes of ancient Egypt.'"

It is stated in the *Family Magazine*, (c), as follows:—

"Public attention has been recently excited respecting the ruins of an ancient city found in Guatamala. It would seem that these ruins are now being explored, and much curious and valuable matter in a literary and historical point of view is anticipated. We deem the present a most auspicious moment, now that the public attention is turned to the subject, to spread its contents before our readers, as an introduction to future discoveries during the researches now in progress." (d)

(c) No. 34, page 266, for 1833. (d) Catherwood and Stephens afterwards ~~blished the result of their explorations of these ruins.

The following are some of the particulars, as related by Captain Del Rio, who partially examined them, as above related, in 1787:—

"From Palenque, the last town northward in the province of *Ciudad Real de Chiapa*, taking a south-westerly direction and ascending a ridge of highland that divides the kingdom of Guatamala from Yucatan, at the distance of six miles, is the little river *Micol* whose waters flow in a westerly direction, and unite with the great river *Tulijah*, which bends its course towards the province of *Tobasco*. Having passed Micol, the ascent begins, and at half a league, or a mile and a half, the traveller crosses a little stream called Otolum; from this point heaps of stone ruins are discovered, which render the roads very difficult for another half league, when you gain the height whereon the stone houses are situated, being still fourteen in number in one place, some more dilapidated than others, yet still having many of their apartments perfectly discernible.

"A rectangular area three hundred yards in breadth by four hundred and fifty in length, which is a fraction over fifty-six rods wide, and eighty-four rods long, being, in the whole circuit, two hundred and eighty rods, which is three-fourths of a mile, and a trifle over, This area presents a plain at the base of the highest mountain forming the ridge. In the centre of the plain is situated the largest of the structures which has as yet been discovered among these ruins. It stands on a mound or pyramid twenty yards high, which is sixty feet, or nearly four rods in perpendicular altitude, which gives it a lofty and beautiful majesty, as if it were a temple suspended in the sky. This is surrounded by other edifices, namely; five to the northward, four to southward, one to the south-west, and three to the eastward,—fourteen it all. In all directions, the fragments of other fallen buildings are seen extending along the mountain that stretches east and west either way from these buildings, as if it were the great temple of worship, or their government house, around which they built their city, and where dwelt their kings and officers of state. At this place was found a subterranean stone aqueduct, of great solidity and durability, which in its course passes beneath the largest building."

Let it be understood, this city of Otolum, the ruins of which are so immense, is in North, not South America, in the same latitude with the island of Jamaica, which is about eighteen degrees north of the equator, being on the highest ground between the northern end of the Caribbean Sea and the Pacific Ocean, where the continent narrows towards the Isthmus of Panama, and is about eight hundred miles south of New Orleans.

The discovery of these ruins, and also of many others equally wonderful in the same country, has aroused the attention of the schools of Europe, who had denied that America could boast of her antiquities. But these immense ruins, have been explored under the direction of Catherwood and

Stephens, a history of which, in detail, has been published in two large volumes. A gentleman who was living near the town of Cincinnati, in 1826, on the upper level, had occasion to sink a well for his accommodation, who persevered in digging to the depth of eighty feet without finding water, but still persisting in the attempt, his workmen found themselves obstructed by a substance which resisted their labor, though evidently not stone. They cleared the surface and sides from the earth bedded around it, when there appeared the stump of a tree, three feet in diameter, and two feet high, which had been cut down with an axe. The marks of the axe were yet visible. It was nearly of the color and apparent character of coal, but had not the friable and fusible quality of that substance. Ten feet below the water sprang up, and the well is now in constant supply and high repute. (e)

In Morse's Universal Geography, volume 1, page 142, the discovery of two stumps is described as follows:—

"In digging a well in Cincinnati, the stump of a tree was found in a sound state, ninety feet below the surface; and in digging another well, at the same place, another stump was found, at ninety-four feet below the surface, which had evident marks of the axe; and on the top there appeared as if some iron tool had been consumed by rust."

We might fill a volume with accounts of American antiquities, all going to show that this country has been inhabited by a people who possessed a knowledge of the arts and sciences, who built cities, cultivated the earth, and who were in possession of a written language. But the things which we have introduced, are abundantly sufficient for our purpose. If a few characters in Hebrew have been found in the earth in America, written on parchment, then it is just as easy to admit that a whole volume has been found in the earth in America, written on plates, in "Reformed Egyptian" characters. The astonishing fact of the stumps being found eighty or ninety feet under ground at Cincinnati, and similar discoveries in many other parts of North and South America, such as buried cities, and other antiquities, all go to prove that there has been a mighty convulsion and revolution, not only of nations, but of nature; and such a convulsion as is no where else so reasonably accounted for as in the following extraordinary and wonderful account of events, which transpired in this country during the crucifixion of the Messiah, which we extract from the Book of Mormon, (f)

(e) See Priest's Antiquities, p. 125. (f) Book of Nephi 4 : 2–10.

"And it came to pass in the thirty and fourth year, in the first month, in the fourth day of the month, there arose a great storm, such an one as never had been known in all the land; and there was also a great and terrible tempest; and there was terrible thunder, insomuch that it did shake the whole earth as if it was about to divide asunder; and there were exceeding sharp lightnings, such as had never been known in all the land. And the city of Zarahemla did take fire; and the city of Moroni did sink into the depths of the sea, and the inhabitants thereof were drowned; and the earth was carried up upon the city of Moronihah, that in the place of the city thereof, there became a great mountain; and there was a great and terrible destruction in the land southward. But behold, there was a more great and terrible destruction in the land northward: for behold, the whole face of the land was changed, because of the tempest, and the whirlwinds, and the thunderings, and the lightnings, and the exceeding great quaking of the whole earth; and the highways were broken up, and the level roads were spoiled, and many smooth places became rough, and many great and notable cities were sunk, and many were burned, and many were shook till the buildings thereof had fallen to the earth, and the inhabitants thereof were slain, and the places were left desolate; and there were some cities which remained; but the damage thereof was exceeding great, and there were many in them who were slain; and there were some who were carried away in the whirlwind; and whither they went, no man knoweth, save they know that they were carried away; and thus the face of the whole earth became deformed, because of the tempests, and the thunderings, and the lightnings, and the quaking of the earth. And behold, the rocks were rent in twain; they were broken up upon the face of the whole earth, insomuch that they were found in broken fragments, and in seams, and in cracks, upon all the face of the land.

"And it came to pass that when the thunderings, and the lightnings, and the storm, and the tempest, and the quakings of the earth did cease—for behold, they did last for about the space of three hours; and it was said by some that the time was greater; nevertheless, all these great and terrible things were done in about the space of three hours; and then behold, there was darkness upon the face of the land.

"And it came to pass that there was thick darkness upon all the face of the land, insomuch that the inhabitants thereof who had not fallen, could feel the vapor of darkness; and there could be no light, because of the darkness; neither candles, neither torches; neither could there be fire kindled with their fine and exceeding dry wood, so that there could not be any light at all; and there was not any light seen, neither fire nor glimmer, neither the sun, nor the moon, nor the stars, for so great were the mists of darkness which were upon the face of the land.

"And it came to pass that it did last for the space of three days, that there was no light seen; and there was great mourning, and howling, and weeping among all the people continually; yea, great were the groanings of the people because of the darkness and the great destructions which had come upon them. And in one place they were heard to cry, saying, O that we had repented before this great and terrible day, and then would our brethren have been spared, and they would not have been burned in that great city Zarahemla. And in another place they were heard to cry and mourn, saying, O that we had repented before this great and terrible day, and had not killed and stoned the prophets, and cast them out; then would our mothers, and our fair daughters, and our children have been spared, and not have been buried up in that great city Moronihah; and thus were the howlings of the people great and terrible.

"And it came to pass that there was a voice heard among all the inhabitants of the earth upon all the face of this land, crying, Wo, wo, wo unto this people; wo unto the inhabitants of the whole earth, except they shall repent, for the devil laugheth and his angels rejoice, because of the slain of the fair sons and daughters of my people; and it is because of their iniquity and abominations that they are fallen. Behold, the great city Zarahemla have I burned with fire, and the inhabitants thereof. And behold, that great city Moroni have I caused to be sunk in the depths of the sea, and the inhabitants thereof to be drowned. And behold, the great city Moronihah have I covered with earth, and the inhabitants thereof, to hide their iniquities and their abominations from before my face, and the blood of the prophets and the saints shall not come any more unto me against them. And behold, the city of Gilgal have I caused to be sunk, and the inhabitants thereof to be buried up in the depths of the earth; yea, and the city Onihah, and the inhabitants thereof, and the city of Mocum, and the inhabitants thereof, and the city of Jerusalem, and the inhabitants thereof, and waters have I caused to come up in the stead thereof, to hide their wickedness and abominations from before my face, that the blood of the prophets and the saints shall not come up any more unto me against them. And behold, the city of Gadiandi, and the city of Gadiomnah, and the city of Jacob, and the city of Gimgimno, all these have I caused to be sunk, and made hills and valleys in the places thereof, and the inhabitants thereof have I buried up in the depths of the earth, to hide their wickedness and abominations from before my face, that the blood of the prophets and the saints should not come up any more unto me against them. And behold, the great city Jacobugath, which was inhabited by the people of the king of Jacob, have I caused to be burned with fire, because of their sins and their wickedness, which was above all the wickedness of the whole earth, because of their secret murders and combinations; for it was they that did destroy the peace of my people and the government of the land: therefore I did cause them to be burned, to destroy them from before my face, that the blood of the prophets and the saints should not come up unto me any more against them. And behold, the city of Laman, and the city of Josh, and the city of Gad, and the city of Kishkumen, have I caused to be burned with fire, and the inhabitants thereof, because of their wickedness in casting out the prophets, and stoning those whom I did send to declare unto them concerning their wickedness and their abominations; and because they did cast them all out, that there were none righteous among them, I did send down fire and destroy them, that their wickedness and abominations might be hid from before my face, that the blood of the prophets and the saints whom I sent among them, might not cry unto me from the ground against them; and many great destructions have I caused to come upon this land, and upon this people, because of their wickedness and their abominations.

"O all ye that are spared, because ye were more righteous than they, will ye not now return unto me, and repent of your sins, and be converted, that I may heal you? Yea, verily I say unto you, if ye will come unto me, ye shall have eternal life. Behold, mine arm of mercy is extended towards you, and whosoever will come, him will I receive; and blessed are those who come unto me. Behold I am Jesus Christ, the Son of God. I created the heavens and the earth, and all things that in them are. I was with the Father from the beginning. I am in the Father, and the Father in me; and in me hath the Father glorified his name. I came unto my own, and my own received me not. And the scriptures, concerning my coming, are fulfilled. And as many as have received me, to them have I given to become the sons of God; and even so will I to as many as shall believe on my name, for, behold, by me redemption cometh, and in me is the law of Moses fulfilled. I am the light and the life of the world. I am Alpha and Omega, the beginning and the end. And ye shall offer up unto me no more the shedding of blood; yea, your sacrifices and your burnt offerings shall be done away, for I will accept none of your sacrifices and your burnt offerings; and ye shall offer for a sacrifice unto me a broken heart and a contrite spirit. And whoso cometh unto me with a broken heart and a contrite spirit, him will I baptize with fire and with the Holy Ghost, even as the Lamanites, because of their faith in me, at the time of their conversion, were baptized with fire, and with the Holy Ghost, and they knew it not. Behold, I have come unto the world to bring redemption unto the world, to save the world from sin; therefore whoso repenteth and cometh unto me as a little child, him will I receive; for of such is the kingdom of God. Behold, for such I have laid down my life, and have taken it up again; therefore repent, and come unto me ye ends of the earth, and be saved.

"And now behold, it came to pass that all the people of the land did hear these sayings; and did witness of it. And after these sayings there was silence in the land for the space of many hours; for so great was the astonishment of the people that they did cease lamenting and howling for the loss of their kindred which had been slain; therefore there was silence in the land for the space of many hours.

"And it came to pass that there came a voice again unto the people, and all the people did hear, and did witness of it, saying, O ye people of these great cities which have fallen, who are descendants of Jacob; yea, who are of the house of Israel, how oft have I gathered you as a hen gathereth her chickens under her wings, and have nourished you. And again, how oft would I have gathered you, as a hen gathereth her chickens under her wings; yea, O ye people of the house of Israel, who have fallen; yea, O ye people of the house of Israel; ye that dwell at Jerusalem, as ye that have fallen; yea, how oft would I have gathered you as a hen gathereth her chickens, and ye would not. O ye house of Israel, whom I have spared, how oft will I gather you as a hen gathereth her chickens under her wings, if ye will repent and return unto me with full purpose of heart. But if not, O house of Israel, the places of your dwellings shall become desolate, until the time of the fulfilling of the covenant to your fathers.

"And now it came to pass that after the people had heard these words, behold they began to weep and howl again, because of the loss of their kindred and friends. And it came to pass that thus did the three days pass away. And it was in the morning, and the darkness dispersed from off the face of the land, and the earth did cease to tremble, and the rocks did cease to rend, and the dreadful groanings did cease, and all the tumultuous noises did pass away, and the earth did cleave together again, that it stood, and the mourning and the weeping, and the wailing of the people who were spared alive, did cease; and their mourning was turned into joy, and their lamentations into the praise and thanksgiving unto the Lord Jesus Christ, their Redeemer. And thus far were the scriptures fulfilled, which had been spoken by the prophets."

Here then is an account which shows clearly and definitely how and when the American antiquities became buried; how the stumps of trees were placed eighty or ninety feet under ground; how cities were sunk, and overwhelmed; how mountains fell and valleys rose; how the rocks were rent, and how the whole face of the continent became altered and deformed. We now close this subject by saying to all people, that if they wish information on the antiquities of America; if they wish historical, prophetical, or doctrinal information of the highest importance, let them carefully read the Book of Mormon.

―――――◆―◆―◆―――――

## CHAPTER V.

THE RESURRECTION OF THE SAINTS, AND THE RESTORATION

OF ALL THINGS SPOKEN BY THE PROPHETS.

This is one of the most important subjects which the human mind can contemplate; one, however neglected at the present time, which was once the ground work of the faith, hope, and joy of the Saints. It was a correct understanding of, and firm belief in this subject, that influenced all their movements. Their minds once fastened upon it, they could not be shaken from their purpose; their faith was firm, their joy constant, and their hope like an anchor to the soul, both sure and steadfast, reaching to that within the veil. It was this that enabled them to rejoice in the midst of tribulation, persecution, sword and flame: and in view of this, they took joyfully the spoiling of their goods, and gladly wandered as strangers, and pilgrims on the earth; for they sought a country, a city, and an inheritance, that none but a Saint ever thought of, understood, or even hoped for. Now we can never understand precisely what is meant by restoration unless we understand what is lost or taken away; for instance, when we offer to restore any thing to a man, it is as much as to say he once possessed it, but had lost it, and that we propose to replace, or put him in possession of that which he once had; therefore when a Prophet speaks of the restoration of all things, he means that all things have undergone a change, but are to be again restored to the primitive order in which they once existed.

First then, it becomes necessary for us to take a view of creation, as it rolled in purity from the hand of its Creator; and if we can discover the state in which it then existed, and understand the changes that have taken place since, we shall then be able to understand what is to be restored; and our minds being thus prepared, we will be looking for the very things which shall come, and we will be in no danger of lifting our puny arms in ignorance, to oppose the things of God.

When God had created the heavens and the earth, and separated the light from the darkness, His next great commandment was to the waters:—

"And God said, Let the waters under the heaven be gathered together unto *one* place, and let the dry land appear: and it was so." (*g*)

From this we learn that the waters which are now divided into oceans, seas, and lakes, were then all gathered together into *one* ocean; and consequently that the land which is now torn asunder, and divided into continents and islands, almost innumerable, was then *one* vast continent, or body, not separated as it now is.

Second, we hear the Lord God pronounced the earth, as well as every thing else, very good. From this we learn that there were no deserts, nor barren places; no stagnant swamps, no rough, broken, rugged hills, no vast mountains covered with eternal snow, and that no part of it was located in the frigid zone, so as to render its climate dreary and unproductive, subject to eternal frost or everlasting chains of ice,

Where no sweet flowers, the dreary landscape cheer,
Nor plenteous harvests, crown the passing year;

but the whole earth was probably one vast plain, or interspersed with gently rising hills, and sloping vales, well calculated for cultivation; while its climate was delightfully varied, without any extremely hot, cold, wet, or dry weather, which only tended to crown the varied year with a greater variety of

(*g*) Gen. 1 : 9.

productions; all for the good of man, or animals, fowls or creeping things; while, from the flowery plain, or spicy grove, sweet odors were wafted on every breeze; and all the vast creation breathed nought but health, and peace, and joy.

Next we learn from Genesis, that,—

"God said, Behold I have given you *every* herb bearing seed, which is upon the face of *all* the earth; and every tree in the which is the fruit of a tree, yielding seed; to you it shall be for meat; and to every beast of the earth, and to every fowl of the air, and to every thing that creepeth upon the earth, wherein there is life; I have given every green herb for meat; and it was so." (*h*)

From these verses we learn that the earth yielded no nauseous weeds, no poisonous plants, no thorns or thistles; indeed every thing that grew, was just calculated for the food of man or beast, fowl or creeping thing; and their food was all vegetable; and flesh and blood were never sacrificed to glut their souls, or gratify their appetites; the beasts of the earth were all in perfect harmony with each other; the lion ate straw like the ox, the wolf dwelt with the lamb, the leopard lay down with the kid, the cow and bear fed together in the same pasture, while their young ones reposed in perfect security, under the shade of the same trees; all was peace and harmony, and nothing to hurt nor disturb in all the holy mountain.

And, to crown the whole, man was created in the image of God, and exalted in dignity and power, having dominion over all the vast number of animated beings which covered the earth, while at the same time he inhabited a beautiful and well watered garden, in the midst of which stood the tree of life, to which he had free access; while he stood in the presence of his Maker, conversed with Him face to face, and gazed upon His glory without a dimming vail between.

O reader, contemplate for a moment this beautiful creation, clothed with peace and plenty; the earth teeming with harmless animals, rejoicing over all the plain; the air swarming with delightful birds, whose never ceasing notes filled the air with varied melody, and all in subjection to their rightful sovereign, who rejoiced over them; while a delightful garden stood as the capital of creation, and man seated on the throne of this vast empire, swaying his sceptre over all the earth with undisputed right; while legions of angels encamped round about him, and joined their glad voices in grateful songs of praise and shouts of joy; while not a sigh nor groan was heard throughout the earth; no death, no sorrow, no tears, no weeping, no pain nor sickness; no contentions, wars nor bloodshed; but peace crowned the seasons as they rolled; and life, joy, and love reigned over all His works. But how changed is the scene since that time.

Let us trace some of the important changes which have taken place, and the causes which have conspired to reduce the earth and its inhabitants to their present state.

First, man, by giving heed to temptation, fell from his standing before God; and this fall affected the whole creation, as well as man, and caused various changes to take place. Man was banished from the presence of his Creator, and a vail was drawn between them, and he was banished from the garden of Eden, to till the earth, (which was then cursed for man's sake, and begun to bring forth thorns and thistles), and with the sweat of his face, and in sorrow, he was to eat of it all the days of his life, and finally return to dust. But as to Eve, her curse was a great multiplicity of sorrow and conception; and between her seed, and the seed of the serpent, there was to be a constant enmity; it should bruise the serpent's head, and the serpent should bruise his heel.

Reader, contemplate the change. The world which had until then been so beautiful, had now become the abode of sorrow and toil, of death and mourning. The earth groaned with its production of thorns and thistles, and man and beast were at enmity; the serpent slyly crept away, fearing lest his head should get the deadly bruise; and man startled amid the thorny path, in fear lest the serpent's fangs should pierce his heel; while the lamb yielded his blood upon the smoking altar, and soon man began to persecute, hate, and murder his fellow, until at length the earth was filled with violence, all flesh became corrupt, the powers of darkness prevailed, and it repented Noah that God had made man, and it grieved him at his heart, for the Lord came out in vengeance, and cleansed the earth by water. How far the flood may have contributed to produce the various changes, as to the division of the earth into broken fragments, islands, and continents, mountains and valleys, we have not been informed, yet the change must have been considerable. But after the flood, in the days of Peleg, the earth was divided. (*i*) It is a short history, to be sure, of so great an event, but still it will account for the mighty revolution, which rolled the sea from its own place in the

(*h*) Gen. 1 : 29, 30.

north, and brought it to interpose between different portions of the earth, which were parted asunder, and moved into something near their present form; this, together with the earthquakes, revolutions and commotions, which have since taken place, have all contributed to reduce the face of the earth to its present state, while the great curses, which have fallen upon different portions because of the wickedness of men, will account for stagnant swamps, the sunken lakes, the dead seas, and great deserts. Witness for instance the denunciations of the prophets upon Babylon, how it was to become perpetual desolations, a den of wild beasts, a dwelling of unclean and hateful birds, a place for owls; and should never be inhabited, but should lie desolate from generation to generation. Witness also the plains of Sodom, filled with towns, cities, and flourishing gardens, well watered. Witness the land of Palestine; in the days of Solomon it was capable of sustaining millions of people, besides a surplus of wheat and other productions, which were exchanged with the neighboring nations; but it has been desolate ever since the Jews were driven from that land until recently. *Now its former fertility is restored.* And when I cast mine eyes over our own land and see the numerous swamps, lakes, and ponds of stagnant waters, together with the vast mountains and innumerable rough places, while rocks have been rent, and torn asunder, from centre to circumference, I exclaim, Whence all this! But, when I read the Book of Mormon, it informs me that while Christ was crucified by the Jews, this whole American continent was shaken to its foundation, that many cities were sunk, and waters came up in their places; that the rocks were rent in twain; that mountains were thrown up to an exceeding height, and other mountains became valleys; the level roads spoiled, and the whole face of the land changed. I then exclaim, These things are no longer a mystery. I have now learned to account for the many wonders which I every where behold throughout our whole country. When I am passing a ledge of rocks, and see that they have all been rent and torn asunder, while some huge fragments are found deeply imbedded in the earth, some rods from whence they were torn, I exclaim with astonishment, These were the groans, the convulsive throes of agonizing nature, while the Son of God suffered upon the cross.

Men have also degenerated, and greatly changed, as well a the earth. The sins, the abominations, and the many evil habits of the latter ages have added to the miseries, toils and sufferings of human life. The idleness, extravagance, pride, covetousness, drunkenness, and other abominations, which are characteristics of the latter times, have all combined to sink mankind to the lowest stage of wretchedness and degradation; while priestcraft and false doctrines have greatly tended to lull mankind to sleep, and to cause them to rest incomparably short of the powers and attainments which the ancients did enjoy, and which are alone calculated to exalt the intellectual powers of the human mind; to establish noble and generous sentiments; to enlarge the heart, and to expand the soul to its utmost capacity. Many of the ancient Saints conversed with Jehovah; learned lessons from the angels; received instruction by the Holy Ghost, in dreams by night and visions by day; until at length the vail was taken off, and they were permitted to gaze with wonder and admiration upon things past and future; yea, even to soar aloft amid unnumbered worlds; while the vast expanse of eternity stood open before them, and they contemplated the mighty works of the Great I AM, until they knew as they were known, and saw as they were seen.

Compare this intelligence with the smatterings of education and worldly wisdom, which seem to satisfy the narrow mind of man in our generation; and, having seen the two contrasted, you will be able to form some idea of the vast elevation from which man has fallen; you will also learn how very far beneath his former glory and dignity he is now living; and your heart will mourn, and be exceedingly sorrowful, when you contemplate him in his low estate and think he is your brother; and you will be ready to exclaim, O man! how art thou fallen! Once thou wast the favorite of Heaven; thy Maker delighted to converse with thee; and angels, and the spirits of just men made perfect were thy companions; but now thou art degraded and brought down. Well did the Apostle Peter say of you, that you know nothing only what you know naturally; as brute beasts made to be taken and destroyed, and thus you perish from generation to generation, while all creation groans under its pollution, and death and sorrow, mourning and weeping, fill up the measure of the days of man.

The Apostle Peter, while preaching to the Jews, said,—

"And he shall send Jesus Christ, which before was preached unto you, whom the heavens must receive until the times of restitution, [restoration] of all things which God hath spoken, by the mouth of all the holy prophets, since the world began." (*i*)

(*i*) Acts 3 : 21.

It appears from the above, that all the holy prophets since Adam have had their eyes upon a certain time, when all things should be restored to their primitive beauty and excellence. And we also learn that the time of restitution was to be at or near the time of Christ's second coming, for the heavens are to receive Him until the times of the restitution, and then the Father shall send Him again to the earth.

"Comfort ye, comfort ye my people saith your God. Speak ye comfortably to Jerusalem, and cry unto her, that her warfare is accomplished, that her iniquity is pardoned: for she hath received of the Lord's hand double for all her sins. The voice of him that crieth in the wilderness, prepare ye the way of the Lord, make straight in the desert a highway for our God. Every valley shall be exalted, and every mountain and hill shall be made low: and the crooked shall be made straight, and the rough places plain: and the glory of the Lord shall be reavealed, and all flesh shall see it together; for the mouth of the Lord hath spoken it." (j)

From these verses we learn: first, that the voice of one shall be heard in the wilderness, to prepare the way of the Lord, just at the time when Jerusalem has been trodden down of the Gentiles long enough to have received at the Lord's hand double for all her sins, when the warfare of Jerusalem is accomplished and her iniquities pardoned; then shall this proclamation be made as it was before by John, yea, a second proclamation, to prepare the way of the Lord for His second coming; and about that time every valley shall be exalted, and every mountain and hill shall be made low, and the crooked shall be made straight, and rough places plain, and then the glory of the Lord shall be revealed, and all flesh shall see it together, for the mouth of the Lord hath spoken it. These mighty revolutions will restore the face of the earth to its former beauty.

In the thirty-fifth chapter of Isaiah we read of the Lord's second coming, and of the mighty works which will attend it. The barren deserts will abound with pools and springs of living water, and produce grass, with flowers blooming as the rose, and that too about the time of the coming of their God with vengeance and recompense, which must allude to his second coming; and Israel is to come at the time to Zion with songs of everlasting joy, and sorrow and sighing shall flee away. Thus the curse will be taken off from the deserts, and they will become fruitful, well watered countries.

The islands will return again to the continents from which they were separated. For this refer to the sixth chapter and

(j) Isaiah 40: 1-5.

fourteenth verse of Revelations: "And every mountain and island were moved out of their places."

From this we learn that they will move somewhere, and as it will be the time of restoring what had been lost, they will accordingly return and join themselves to the land from whence they came.

"The earth shall move out of her place, and be like a chased roe which no man taketh up." (*k*)

"Thou shalt no more be termed forsaken; neither shall thy land any more be termed desolate; but thou shalt be termed Hepzibah, and thy land Beulah: for the Lord delighteth in thee, and thy land shall be married." (*l*)

First, then, the earth will be like a chased roe, and in the second place it will be married. From this and various other passages of scripture, we learn that the continents and islands will be united in one, as they were in the morn of creation, and the sea shall retire and be gathered to its own place, where it was in that day; and all these scenes shall take place during the mighty convulsion of nature, about the time of the coming of the Lord.

> Behold! the Mount of Olives rend in twain;
> While on its top He sets His feet again,
> The islands at His word obedient flee;
> While to the north He rolls the mighty sea,
> Restores the earth in one as at the first;
> With all its blessings, and removes the curse.

The earth will then be restored to the same glorious state in which it first existed; the mountains leveled, the valleys exalted, the rough places made smooth, the deserts fruitful, the continents and all the islands brought together, causing the curse to be taken off, that it shall no longer produce noxious weeds and thorns and thistles. The brute creation will also be restored to its former state of peace and glory, and all enmity will cease from off the earth. But this will never be done until there is a general destruction poured out upon all men who know not God and who obey not the gospel, which will entirely cleanse the earth, and sweep all wickedness from its face. This will be done by the rod of His mouth, and by the breath of His lips, or in other words by a fire as universal as the flood. Isaiah said:

"With righteousness shall he judge the poor, and reprove with equity for the meek of the earth, and with the breath of his lips shall he slay the wicked. The wolf shall dwell with the lamb, and the leopard shall lie down with the kid, and the calf, and the young lion, and the fatling

(*k*) Isaiah 13:13, 14. (*l*) Isaiah 62:4.

together; and a little child shall lead them. And the cow and the bear shall feed; their young ones shall lie down together; and the lion shall eat straw like the ox. And the sucking child shall play on the hole of the asp, and the weaned child shall put his hand on the cockatrice's den. They shall not hurt nor destroy in all my holy mountain; for the earth shall be full of the knowledge of the Lord, as the waters cover the sea." (*m*)

The earth being cleansed and glorified with the knowledge of God as the waters cover the sea, and God having poured out his Spirit upon all flesh, man and beast will become peaceable, as they were in the beginning, and they will feed on vegetable food only, while nothing will be left to hurt or destroy in all the vast creation. The prophets give us many glorious descriptions of the enjoyments of the inhabitants of the earth.

"They shall build houses and inhabit them; they shall plant vineyards and drink the wine of them; they shall plant gardens and eat the fruit of them; they shall not build and another inhabit; they shall not plant and another eat; for as the days of a tree, are the days of my people; and mine elect shall long enjoy the work of their hands. They shall not labor in vain, nor bring forth in trouble; for they are the seed of the Lord, and their offspring with them; and it shall come to pass that before they call I will answer, and while they are yet speaking I will hear." (*n*)

In this state of happy existence it seems that all people will live to the full age of a tree, and this, too, without pain or sorrow; and whatsoever they ask will be immediately answered, and even all their wants will be anticipated. Of course then, none of them will sleep in the dust, for they will prefer to be translated, that is changed in the twinkling of an eye, from mortality to immortality, after which they will continue to reign with Jesus on the earth.

Thus we have traced the prophet through the varying scenes which conspire to restore the earth and its inhabitants to that state of perfection in which they first existed, and in which they will exist during the sabbath of creation.

Having seen all things restored among the living we now enquire after those who sleep in the dust. In order to understand precisely the nature of their restoration we must ascertain the particulars concerning the resurrection of Jesus; for he was the pattern after which all his saints will be raised. We recollect, first, that he was clothed upon with flesh, and blood, and bones, like other men, and every way subject to hunger, thirst, pain, weariness, sickness and death, like any

(*m*) Isaiah 11 : 4, 9.   (*n*) Isaiah 65 : 21-24.

other person, with this difference, that he was capable of enduring more than any other human body. Second, this same body was hung upon the cross, torn with nails, which were driven through his hands and feet; his side was pierced with a spear and there came out blood and water. Third, this same body being entirely lifeless, like any other corpse, was taken, without a bone being broken, and carefully wrapped in linen and laid in the tomb, where it continued for three days. Then, early in the morning, the women came to the sepulchre, and his disciples also, and found the linen clothes lying useless, and the napkin which was about his head carefully folded and laid by itself, but the body which had lain there was gone. From all these circumstances we discover that the same flesh and bones which were laid in the tomb were actually reanimated, and did arise and lay aside the linen which was no longer needed; and Jesus Christ came forth triumphant from the mansions of the dead, possessing the same body which had been born of a woman, and which had been crucified. But no blood flowed in his veins, for blood was the natural life in which were the principles of mortality, and a man restored to flesh and blood would be mortal, and consequently again subject to death, which was not the case with our Savior, although he had flesh and bones after he rose; for, when he appeared to his disciples, and they were afraid, supposing it was only a spirit, he, in order to show them their mistake, said:

"Handle me and see, for a spirit hath not flesh and bones as you see me have." (*o*)

And calling for something to eat, he was provided with a piece of broiled fish and an honey comb, which he did eat. And even afterwards Thomas was invited to put his finger into the prints of the nails in his hands and feet, and to thrust his hand into his side. From this it is evident that he not only possessed the same body, but also the same wounds continued to show themselves for a witness, and will continue to until he comes again, when the Jews will look upon Him whom they have pierced, and enquire: "What are the wounds in his hands and in his feet?" O ye hard hearted children of men, your eyes will behold him who was crucified for your sins; then shall ye see that the resurrection of the dead is a reality, something tangible, and that eternity is not a land of shades, nor a world of phantoms, as some suppose.

(*o*) Luke 24 ; 39.

Jesus, after the resurrection, was found in the humble work of broiling fish, and calling his disciples to come and dine. O what simplicity, what love, what condescension! Wonder O heavens! Be astonished O earth! Behold the Redeemer, clothed upon with immortality, and yet seated by a fire of coals, in the open air with his brethren, humbly partaking of a meal of fish actually prepared by his own hands. O ye great and noble of the earth, who roll in luxury and refinement. O ye priests, who are loaded with the honors, titles, dignities, riches, and splendor of the world, here is a lesson for you which should make you blush. Boast no more of being followers of the meek and lowly Jesus!

It having been proved that our Savior rose from the dead, with the same body which was crucified, possessing flesh and bones, and that he ate and drank with His disciples, this puts the matter forever at rest respecting the resurrection of the Saints. But, if more proof were wanting, we have it in the prophecy of Job, before quoted in this work, where he declares that his Redeemer will stand in the latter day upon the earth, and he shall see him in the flesh, though worms should destroy the body which he then had. The fact is, the Saints will again receive their bodies, every joint in its perfect frame, being clothed upon with flesh, sinews, and skin, like as we now are; the whole becoming immortal, no more to see corruption, being clothed with a white robe of fine linen, suitable for immortality to wear. Well did the apostle say, "in heaven we have a more enduring *substance*," (not shadow). In the vision of Ezekiel the prophet was carried away in the Spirit, and a valley of dry bones was presented before him, and they were very numerous and very dry; and, while he stood musing and contemplating the awful scene, a very wonderful question was proposed to him:

"Son of man, can these bones live? And I answered, O Lord God thou knowest. Again he said unto me, Prophesy upon these bones, and say unto them, O ye dry bones, hear the word of the Lord." (*p*)

So he prophesied as he was commanded, and, as he prophesied, there was a noise, and behold a shaking, and the bones came together, bone to his bone, and the sinews and the flesh came upon them, and the skin covered them. And again he prophesied to the winds, saying, "Come from the four winds, O breath, and breathe upon these slain that they may live," and the breath entered into them, and they lived and stood upon their feet, an exceeding great army.

We have heard many comments upon this vision. Some compare it to sinners being converted, and some to the body of Christ, the church, when dead as to spiritual gifts; but the church becoming dead, can no longer be said to be the body of Christ, for, when she abides in the true vine, she lives and bears fruit, and is not dead; and where she does not abide in Him she is cast off as a branch, withered and burned, instead of rising again. The Lord's own explanation of this vision in the same chapter, so far surpasses all other comments, that I am inclined to believe it. I therefore write it in preference to the other and run the risk of becoming unpopular by so doing. The Lord says:

"Son of man, these bones are the whole house of Israel; behold, they say, Our bones are dried, and our hope is lost; we are cut off for our parts. Therefore prophesy and say unto them, Thus saith the Lord God: Behold, O my people, I will open your graves, and bring you into the land of Israel. And ye shall know that I am the Lord, when I have opened your graves, O my people, and brought you up out of your graves, and shall put my Spirit in you, and ye shall live, and I shall place you in your own land; then shall ye know that I the Lord have spoken it, and performed it, saith the Lord." (*q*)

All the seed of Israel are to be raised from the dead, and to be brought into the land of Israel, which was given them for an everlasting inheritance. In order to do this, their bones are to be brought together bone to his bone, and every part of their bodies to be reinstated, each in its place; and surely when they stand upon their feet they will make an exceeding great army. Jesus, the King of kings and Lord of lords, will reign in Mount Zion, and in Jerusalem, and before His ancients and the redeemed of all people, gloriously.

> O glorious day! O blessed hope!
> My soul leaps forward at the thought;
> When in that happy, happy land,
> We'll take the ancients by the hand,
> In love and union, hail our friends,
> And death and sorrow have an end.

I no longer marvel when I call to mind that Abraham counted himself a stranger, and a pilgrim, seeking a better country, and a city, whose maker and builder is God. We have discovered the great secret which none but the Saints have understood, but which was well understood by them in all ages of the world; which is this, that man is to dwell in the flesh, upon the earth, with the whole house of Israel, and with all the Saints of the Most High, not only one thousand

(*p*) 37 : 3, 4.

years, but forever. There the Ancient of Days, whose hair is white like pure wool, will sit enthroned in dignity, as the great Patriarch, the mighty Prince, while thousands of thousands stand before him, and ten thousand times ten thousand minister to him. There he will hail all his children who died in the faith of the Messiah; while Abel, Enoch, Noah, Abraham, Job, and Daniel, with all the prophets and apostles, and all the saints of God of all ages, will hail each other in the flesh, and Jesus, the great Messiah, will stand in their midst; and, to crown the whole, he will gird himself, and will administer bread and wine to the whole multitude, all of them clothed in fine linen, clean and white. This is the marriage supper of the Lamb. Blessed are they who shall partake thereof.

Having traced the great restoration of the earth and its inhabitants, until we find them in the full enjoyment of the promises made to their fathers; and, having learned that a future state is not a state of shadows and fables, but a reality, even a more enduring substance, we shall now take a view of the division of their land, and the laying out of their city, even the holy city, where the tabernacle of God and His sanctuary shall be forever more; for, of course, this was the city sought for by Abraham, and by others, who found it not. This view is given in the last chapter of Ezekiel, where he divides the land by lot to the whole twelve tribes, and lays off the city, with its twelve gates, three on each side, lying four square, and the sanctuary in the midst. But, in his forty-seventh chapter, we have a description of a beautiful river, which will issue forth from the eastern front of the temple, from under the sanctuary, and run eastward into the Dead Sea, healing the waters, and causing a great multitude of fishes, so that from Engedi to Eneglaim the fishers spread forth their nets; while the miry places shall not be healed, but shall be given to salt. And, on either side, shall grow all trees for meat, whose leaf shall not fade, nor shall the fruit thereof be consumed; it shall bring forth new fruit according to its months; because their waters will issue out of the sanctuary; and the fruit will be for meat, and the leaf thereof for medicine.

There will be also a city which is called Zion, which will be most beautiful, and the chosen city of God, as the prophet states:

"O thou afflicted, tossed with tempest, and not comforted! behold, I lay thy stones in fair colors, and lay thy foundations with sapphires.

And I will make thy windows of agates, and thy gates of carbuncles, and all thy borders of pleasant stones. And all thy children shall be taught of the Lord; and great shall be the peace of thy children. In righteousness shalt thou be established; thou shalt be far from oppression, for thou shalt not fear; and from terror, for it shall not come near thee. Behold, they shall surely gather together, but not by me; whosoever shall gather together against thee shall fall for thy sake. Behold, I have created the smith that bloweth the coals in the fire, and that bringeth forth an instrument for his work; and I have created the waster to destroy. No weapon that is formed against thee shall prosper; and every tongue that shall rise against thee in judgment thou shalt condemn. This is the heritage of the servants of the Lord, and their righteousness is of me, saith the Lord." (*r*)

From these verses we learn something about the glory of this city, and of the materials of which it will be composed; their stones of fair colors, their foundations of sapphires, their windows of agates, and their gates of carbuncles, and their borders of pleasant stones; all these well calculated to beautify the place of his sanctuary, and to make the place of his feet glorious, as well as to give a lustre and magnificence to the whole city, of which the Gentiles, with all their boasted wealth and grandeur, can form but a faint idea; and then, to mark in the same description, the knowledge, as well as the peace and security of the inhabitants, while they who gather against them to battle are sure to fall for their sake; surely this is the heritage of the servants of the Lord; surely, this is a delightful city, and well worth a pilgrimage like Abraham's. But, in order to form a more striking idea of the prosperity, wealth, beauty, and magnificence, of Zion, we will quote Isaiah, sixtieth chapter:

"Arise, shine; for thy light is come, and the glory of the Lord is risen upon thee. For behold, the darkness shall cover the earth, and gross darkness the people; but the Lord shall arise upon thee, and his glory shall be seen upon thee. And the Gentiles shall come to thy light, and kings to the brightness of thy rising. Lift up thine eyes round about, and see: all they gather themselves together, they come to thee: thy sons shall come from far, and thy daughters shall be nursed at thy side. Then thou shalt see, and flow together, and thine heart shall fear, and be enlarged; because the abundance of the sea shall be converted unto thee, the forces of the Gentiles shall come unto thee. The multitude of camels shall cover thee, the dromedaries of Midian and Ephah; all they from Sheba shall come: they shall bring gold and incense; and they shall shew forth the praises of the Lord. All the flocks of Kedar shall be gathered together unto thee, the rams of Nebaioth shall minister unto thee: they shall come up with acceptance on mine altar, and I will glorify the house of my glory. Who are these that fly as a cloud, and as the doves to their windows? Surely the isles shall

(*r*) Isaiah 54 : 11-17.

wait for me, and the ships of Tarshish first, to bring thy sons from far, their silver and their gold with them, unto the name of the Lord thy God, and to the Holy One of Israel, because he hath glorified thee. And the sons of strangers shall build up thy walls, and their kings shall minister unto thee: for in my wrath I smote thee, but in my favor have I had mercy on thee. Therefore thy gates shall be open continually; they shall not be shut day nor night: that men may bring unto thee the forces of the Gentiles, and that their kings may be brought. For the nation and kingdom that will not serve thee shall perish; yea, those nations shall be utterly wasted. The glory of Lebanon shall come unto thee, the fir-tree, the pine-tree, and box together, to beautify the place of my sanctuary; and I will make the place of my feet glorious. The sons also of them that afflicted thee shall come bending unto thee: and all they that despised thee shall bow themselves down at the soles of thy feet; and they shall call thee The City of the Lord, The Zion of the Holy One of Israel. Whereas thou hast been forsaken and hated, so that no man went through thee, I will make thee an eternal excellency, the joy of many generations. Thou shalt also suck the milk of the Gentiles, and shalt suck the breast of kings: and thou shalt know that I the Lord am thy Savior and thy Redeemer, the Mighty One of Jacob. For brass I will bring gold, and for iron I will bring silver, and for wood brass, and for stones iron; I will also make thy officers peace, and thine exactors righteousness. Violence shall no more be heard in thy land, wasting nor destruction within thy borders; but thou shalt call thy walls Salvation and thy gates Praise. The sun shall be no more thy light by day; neither for brightness shall the moon give light unto thee; but the Lord shall be unto thee an everlasting light, and thy God thy glory. Thy sun shall no more go down; neither shall thy moon withdraw itself; for the Lord shall be thine everlasting light, and the days of thy mourning shall be ended. Thy people also shall be all righteous; they shall inherit the land forever, the branch of my planting, the work of my hands, that I may be glorified. A little one shall become a thousand, and a small one a strong nation; I the Lord will hasten it in his time."

In this chapter we learn: First, that there is a city to be built in the last days, unto which not only Israel, but all the nations of the Gentiles are to flow; and that the nation and kingdom that will not serve that city shall perish and be utterly wasted. Second, that the name of that city will be Zion, the city of the Lord. Third, that it is to be the place of his sanctuary, and the place of his feet. Fourth, that the best of lumber, consisting of fir, pine, and boxwood, is to be brought in great plenty to beautify the place of his sanctuary, and to make the place of his feet glorious. Fifth, the precious metals are to abound in such plenty that gold is to be in the place of brass, silver in the place of iron, brass in the place of wood, iron in the place of stones, while their officers are to be peace officers, and their exactors righteous exactors; violence is no more to be heard in the land, wasting nor destruction within their borders; their walls are to be salvation, and their gates praise, while the glory of God in the midst of the city will outshine the sun, and the days of their mourning will be ended; the people will all be righteous, and inherit the land forever, being the branch of the Lord's planting, that He may be glorified. A small one shall become a strong nation, and the Lord will hasten it in his time.

The Psalmist David has told us concerning the time of the building of this city as follows:

"Thou shalt arise, and have mercy upon Zion, for the time to favor her, yea, the set time, is come. For thy servants take pleasure in her stones, and favor the dust thereof. So the heathen shall fear the name of the Lord: and all the kings of the earth thy glory. When the Lord shall build up Zion, he shall appear in his glory. He will regard the prayer of the destitute, and not despise their prayer. This shall be written for generations to come: and the people which shall be created shall praise the Lord. For he hath looked down from the height of his sanctuary: from heaven did the Lord behold the earth; to hear the groaning of the prisoner: to loose those that are appointed to death: to declare the name of the Lord in Zion, and his praise in Jerusalem; when the people are gathered together, and the kingdoms, to serve the Lord." (s)

From this prophecy we learn: First, that there is a set time to build up Zion, or the city of which Isaiah wrote, just before the second coming of Christ, and that when this city shall be built, the Lord will appear in his glory, *and not before*. So from this we affirm, that if such a city is never built, then the Lord will never come. Second, we learn that the people and kingdoms are to be gathered together to serve the Lord, both in Zion and in Jerusalem. Third, we learn that this Psalm was written expressly for the generation to come, and the people which shall be created shall praise the Lord, when they read it and see it fulfilled.

I will now quote a part of the Book of Ether, contained in the Book of Mormon:

"He [Ether] truly told them of all things, from the beginning of man; and that after the waters had receded from off the face of this land, it became a choice land above all other lands, a chosen land of the Lord; wherefore the Lord would have that all men should serve him who dwell upon the face thereof; and that it was the place of the New Jerusalem, which should come down out of heaven, and the holy sanctuary of the Lord. Behold, Ether saw the days of Christ, and he spake concerning a New Jerusalem upon this land; and he spake also concerning the house of Israel, and the Jerusalem from whence Lehi should come; after it should be destroyed it should be built up again a holy city unto the Lord; wherefore it could not be a New Jerusalem, for it had been in a time of old, but it should be built up again, and become a holy city

(s) Psalms 102 : 13–32.

of the Lord: and it should be built unto the house of Israel; and that a New Jerusalem should be built up upon this land, unto the remnant of the seed of Joseph, for which things there has been a type; for as, Joseph brought his father down into the land of Egypt, even so he died there; wherefore the Lord brought a remnant of the seed of Joseph out of the land of Jerusalem, that he might be merciful unto the seed of Joseph, that they should perish not, even as he was merciful unto the father of Joseph, that he should perish not; wherefore the remnant of the house of Joseph shall be built upon this land; and it shall be a land of their inheritance; and they shall build up a holy city unto the Lord like unto the Jerusalem of old; and they shall no more be confounded, until the end come, when the earth shall pass away. And there shall be a new heaven and a new earth; and they shall be like unto the old, save the old have passed away, and all things have become new. And then cometh the New Jerusalem; and blessed are they who dwell therein; for it is they whose garments are white through the blood of the Lamb; and they are they who are numbered among the remnant of the seed of Joseph, who were of the house of Israel. And then also cometh the Jerusalem of old; and the inhabitants thereof. Blessed are they, for they have been washed in the blood of the Lamb; and they are they who were scattered and gathered in from the four quarters of the earth, and from the north countries, and are partakers of the fulfilling of the covenant which God made with their father Abraham. And when these things come, bringeth to pass the scripture which saith, there are they who were first, who shall be last; and there are they who were last who shall be first." (*t*)

From this prophecy we learn: First, that America is a chosen land of the Lord above every other land. Second, that it is the place of the New Jerusalem, which shall come down from God out of heaven, upon the earth, when it will be renewed. Third, that a new Jerusalem will be built in America, to the remnant of Joseph, like unto, or after a pattern similar to the old Jerusalem in the land of Canaan; and that the old Jerusalem will be rebuilt at the same time; and, this being done, both cities will continue in prosperity on the earth, until the last great change, when the heavens and the earth will be renewed. Fourth, we learn that when this change takes place, the two cities will be caught up into heaven, together with the inhabitants thereof, and, being changed and made new, they will descend upon the new earth. The remnant of Joseph, and they who will be numbered among them, will inherit the New Jerusalem. And the remainder of all the tribes of Israel, gathered from the north countries and from the four quarters of the earth, will inhabit the other, and thus, all things being made new, we find those who were once strangers and pilgrims on the earth in possession of that better country, and that city for which they sought.

(*t*) Ether 6 : 1.

John's Revelations inform us how the city will appear after it is made new:

"And I saw a new heaven and a new earth: for the first heaven and the first earth were passed away; and there was no more sea. And I John saw the holy city, New Jerusalem, coming down from God out of heaven, prepared as a bride adorned for her husband. And I heard a great voice out of heaven, saying, Behold the tabernacle of God is with men, and he will dwell with them, and they shall be his people, and God himself shall be with them, and be their God. And God shall wipe away all tears from their eyes; and there shall be no more death, neither sorrow, nor crying, neither shall there be any more pain; for the former things are passed away. And he that sat upon the throne said, Behold, I make all things new. And he said unto me, Write, for these words are true and faithful. And he said unto me, It is done. I am Alpha and Omega, the beginning and the end. I will give unto him that is athirst of the fountain of the water of life freely. He that overcometh shall inherit all things; and I shall be his God and he shall be my son. But the fearful and unbelieving, and the abominable, and murderers, and whoremongers, and sorcerers, and idolaters and all liars, shall have their part in the lake which burneth with fire and brimstone; which is the second death. And there came unto me one of the seven angels, which had the seven vials full of the seven plagues, and talked with me saying, Come hither, I will shew thee the bride, the Lamb's wife. And he carried me away in the Spirit to a great and high mountain, and shewed me that great city, the holy Jerusalem, descending out of heaven from God, having the glory of God: and her light was like unto a stone most precious, even like a jasper stone, clear as crystal; and had a wall great and high, and had twelve gates, and at the gates twelve angels, and names written thereon, which are the names of the twelve tribes of the children of Israel. On the east, three gates; on the north, three gates; on the south, three gates; and on the west, three gates. And the wall of the city had twelve foundations, and in them the name of the twelve apostles of the Lamb. And he that talked with me had a golden reed to measure the city, and the gates thereof, and the walls thereof. And the city lieth four-square, and the length is as large as the breadth: and he measured the city with the reed, twelve thousand furlongs. The length, and the breadth, and the height of it are equal. And he measured the wall thereof, an hundred and forty and four cubits, according to the measure of a man, that is, of the angel. And the building of the wall of it was of jasper: and the city was pure gold, like unto clear glass. And the foundations of the wall of the city were garnished with all manner of precious stones. The first foundation was jasper; the second, sapphire; the third, a chalcedony; the fourth, an emerald; the fifth, sardonyx; the sixth, sardius; the seventh, chrysolite; the eighth, beryl; the ninth, a topaz; the tenth, a chrysoprasus; the eleventh, a jacinth; the twelfth, amethyst. And the twelve gates were twelve pearls; every several gate was of one pearl; and the street of the city was pure gold, as it were transparent glass. And I saw no temple therein: for the Lord God Almighty and the Lamb are the temple of it. And the city had no need of the sun, neither of the moon to shine in it; for the glory of God did lighten it, and the Lamb is the light thereof. And the nations of them which are saved shall walk in the light of it: and the kings of the earth do bring their glory and honor into it. And the gates of it shall not be shut at all by day: for there shall be no night there. And they shall bring the glory and honor of the nations into it. And there shall in no wise enter into it anything that defileth, neither whatsoever worketh abomination, or maketh a lie; but they which are written in the Lamb's book of life.

"And he shewed me a pure river of water of life, clear as crystal, proceeding out of the throne of God and of the Lamb. In the midst of the street of it, and on either side of the river, was there the tree of life, which bare twelve manner of fruits, and yielded her fruit every month; and the leaves of the tree were for the healing of the nations. And there shall be no more curse: but the throne of God and of the Lamb shall be in it; and his servants shall serve him; and they shall see his face: and his name shall be in their foreheads. And there shall be no night there; and they need no candle, neither light of the sun; for the Lord God giveth them light; and they shall reign forever and ever. And he said unto me, These sayings are faithful and true. And the Lord God of the holy prophets sent his angel to show unto his servants the things which must shortly be done. Behold, I come quickly: blessed is he that keepeth the sayings of the prophecy of this book." (*u*)

From this beautiful description we learn that on this new earth there will be no sea, whereas during the thousand years, which we have described, there will be a sea, for we read that after the thousand years are ended the sea will give up the dead which are in it. And, we learn that in this new earth there will be no temple, whereas in the millenium, they who "have washed their robes and made them white in the blood of the Lamb," will "serve Him day and night in His temple." (*v*)

Now of the things of which we have spoken this is the sum: Isaiah and other prophets have given a description of Zion and Jerusalem, as they will be built up in the last days, and as they will continue during the Millenium; and John has given a description of them as they will be after their final change, when they will come down from God out of heaven and rest upon the new earth. But Ether has given us a sketch of them as they are to be, both in their temporal, and in their eternal state; and he has told us plainly concerning their first location, namely: the New Jerusalem in America, inhabited by the remnant of Joseph, and those gathered with them, who will wash their robes and make them white in the blood of the Lamb: and the other Jerusalem in its former place, inhabited by the house of Israel, gathered from the north countries, and from all the countries where they have been scattered, having washed their robes and made them

(*u*) Rev. 21; 22 : 1-7. (*v*) Rev. 7 : 14, 15.

white in the blood of the Lamb. And here is the end of the matter. God will gather them from all the face of the land, and this gathering is clearly predicted in the Book of Mormon, and in other revelations, to be at the place before appointed, and at the time set for its fulfillment; and except the Gentiles repent of all their abominations, and embrace the same covenant, they will soon be utterly destroyed from off the face of this land, as it is written by Isaiah: "The nation and kingdom that will not serve thee shall perish, yea, those nations shall be utterly wasted." In the Book of Mormon it is recorded that Jesus said:

"Verily, I say unto you, I give unto you a sign, that ye may know the time when these things shall be about to take place, that I shall gather in from their long dispersion, my people, O house of Israel, and shall establish again among them my Zion. And behold, this is the thing which I shall give unto you for a sign, for verily I say unto you, that when these things which I declare unto you, and which I shall declare unto you hereafter of myself, and by the power of the Holy Ghost, which shall be given unto you of the Father, shall be made known unto the Gentiles, that they may know concerning this people who are a remnant of the house of Jacob, and concerning this my people who shall be scattered by them; verily, verily, I say unto you, when these things shall be made known unto them of the Father, and shall come forth of the Father, from them unto you, for it is wisdom in the Father that they should be established in this land, and be set up as a free people by the power of the Father, that these things might come forth from them unto a remnant of your seed, that the covenant of the Father may be fulfilled which he hath covenanted with his people, O house of Israel; therefore, when these works, and the works which shall be wrought among you hereafter, shall come forth from the Gentiles unto your seed, which shall dwindle in unbelief because of iniquity; for thus it behooveth the Father that it should come forth from the Gentiles, that he may shew forth his power unto the Gentiles, for this cause, that the Gentiles, if they will not harden their hearts, that they may repent and come unto me, and be baptized in my name, and know of the true points of my doctrine, that they may be numbered among my people, O house of Israel: and when these things come to pass, that thy seed shall begin to know these things, it shall be a sign unto them, that they may know that the work of the Father has already commenced unto the fulfilling of the covenant which he hath made unto the people who are of the house of Israel. And when that day shall come it shall come to pass that kings shall shut their mouths; for that which had not been told them shall they see; and that which they had not heard shall they consider. For in that day, for my sake shall the Father work a work, which shall be a great and a marvelous work among them; and there shall be among them those who will not believe it, although a man shall declare it unto them. But behold the life of my servant shall be in my hand; therefore they shall not hurt him, although he shall be marred because of them. Yet I will heal him, for I will shew unto them that my wisdom is greater than the cunning of the devil. Therefore it shall come to pass, that whosoever will not believe in my words, who am Jesus Christ, whom the Father shall cause him to bring forth unto the Gentiles, and shall give unto him power that he shall bring them forth unto the Gentiles, (it shall be done even as Moses said), they shall be cut off from among my people who are of the covenant; and my people who are a remnant of Jacob, shall be among the Gentiles, yea, in the midst of them, as a lion among the beasts of the forest, as a young lion among the flocks of sheep, who, if he go through both treadeth down and teareth in pieces, and none can deliver. Their hand shall be lifted up upon their adversaries, and all their enemies shall be cut off. Yea, wo be unto the Gentiles, except they repent, for it shall come to pass in that day, saith the Father that I will cut off thy horses out of the midst of thee, and I will destroy thy chariots, and I will cut off the cities of thy land, and throw down all thy strong holds; and I will cut off witchcrafts out of thy land, and thou shalt have no more soothsayers; thy graven images I will also cut off, and thy standing images out of the midst of thee; and thou shalt no more worship the works of thy hands; and I will pluck up the groves out of the midst of thee; so will I destroy thy cities. And it shall come to pass that all lyings, and deceivings, and envyings, and strifes, and priestcrafts and whoredoms shall be done away. For it shall come to pass, saith the Father, that at that day, whosoever will not repent and come unto my beloved Son, them will I cut off from among my people, O house of Israel; and I will execute vengeance and fury upon them, even as upon the heathen, such as they have not heard.

"But if they will repent and hearken unto my words, and harden not their hearts, I will establish my church among them, and they shall come in unto the covenant, and be numbered among this the remnant of Jacob; and also, as many of the house of Israel as shall come, that they may build a city, which shall be called the New Jerusalem; and then shall they assist my people that they may be gathered in, who are scattered upon all the face of the land, in unto the New Jerusalem. And then shall the power of heaven come down among them; and I also will be in the midst, and then shall the work of the Father commence, at that day even when this gospel shall be preached among the remnant of this people. Verily, I say unto you, at that day shall the work of the Father commence among all the dispersed of my people; yea, even the tribes which have been lost, which the Father hath led away out of Jerusalem. Yea, the work shall commence among all the dispersed of my people, with the Father, to prepare the way whereby they may come unto me, that they may call on the Father in my name; yea, and then shall the work commence with the Father, among all nations, in preparing the way whereby his people may be gathered home to the land of their inheritance. And they shall go out from all nations; and they shall not go out in haste, nor go by flight; for I will go before them, saith the Father, and be their reward. (*w*)

O ye remnant of Joseph, your secret *is revealed*, ye who are despised, smitten, scattered, and driven by the Gentiles, from place to place, until you are left few in number. "O thou afflicted, tossed with tempest and not comforted," lift up your heads and rejoice, for your redemption draweth nigh;

(*w*) Book of Nephi, 9th and 10th chapters.

yea, we have found your record; the oracles of God which were committed to your forefathers, and which have been hidden from you for a long time, because of unbelief, behold, they will be restored to you again; then shall you rejoice, for you shall know that it is a blessing from the hand of God, and the scales of darkness shall begin to fall from your eyes, and the Gentiles shall not again have power over you, but you shall be gathered together and be built up, and shall again become a delightsome people, and the time has come; yea, the work has already commenced; for we have seen you gathered together from all parts of our land unto the place which God has appointed for the Gentiles to gather you. The hand of your Great God is in all this; and it was all foretold by your forefathers.

It is with mingled feelings of joy and sorrow that I reflect upon these things; sorrow, when I think how they have been smitten; joy when I reflect upon the happy change that now awaits them; and sorrow again when I turn my thoughts to the awful destruction that awaits the Gentiles, except they repent. But the eternal purposes of Jehovah must roll on until all his promises are fulfilled, and none can hinder: therefore, O God, thy will be done. But, while I still linger upon this subject, with feelings that are easier felt than described, methinks I can almost hear the poor Indian's mournful chant resounding through his native woods. It whispers thus:

> Great Spirit of our fathers, now draw near;
> Pity the red man, to his cries give ear;
> Long hast thou scourged him with thy chastening sore;
> When will thy vengence cease, thy wrath be o'er?
>
> When will the white man's dire ambition cease,
> And let our scattered remnants dwell in peace?
> Or shall we (driven to the western shore)
> Become extinct, and fall to rise no more?
>
> Forbid, Great Spirit! make thy mercy known,
> Reveal thy truth, thy wandering captives own;
> Make bare thine arm of power for our release,
> And o'er the earth extend the reign of peace.

## CHAPTER VI.

#### THE DEALINGS OF GOD WITH ALL NATIONS IN REGARD TO REVELATION.

"And hath made of one blood all nations of men to dwell on all the face of the earth, and hath determined the times before appointed, and the bounds of their habitation: that they should seek the Lord, if haply they might feel after him, and find him, though he be not far from every one of us: for in him we live, and move, and have our being." (x)

In this text we learn, First that all nations are made of one blood. Second, that they are designed to dwell on all the face of the earth, America not excepted. Third, that the Lord had determined the bounds of their habitation, that is he has divided the earth among his children, giving each nation that portion which seemed good to him; for instance, the land of Canaan, to Israel; Mount Seir, to Esau; Arabia, to Ishmael; America, to the remnant of Joseph, etc., as a father parcels off a large tract of land to his several children. And Fourth, he has granted unto all the nations of the earth the privilege of feeling after and finding him; for he is not far from every one of them; whether they are in Asia, Africa, Europe, or America, or even upon the islands of the sea. Now, if any nation in any age of the world, or any part of the earth, should happen to live up to their privilege, what would they obtain? I answer, revelations, for the best of reasons; because no people ever found God in any other way, nor ever will; therefore if they found God, they found him by revelation direct from himself, by his revealing his will to them; and if they did not find him in this way they never knew him; and if they did obtain revelation it was their privilege to write it, and to make a record of the same, and teach it to their children; and this record would be sacred, because it would contain the word of God; and thus it would be holy scripture and as good as the Bible; no matter whether it was written by the Jews, the ten

(x) Acts 17 : 26-28.

tribes, the Nephites, or the Gentiles. I would just as soon have the gospel written by Nephi, Mormon, Moroni, or Alma, as to have the gospel written by Matthew, Mark, Luke, or John. Again, I would just as soon believe a revelation given in America, as to believe a revelation given in Asia; for, if ever a nation failed to get a revelation, it was because they did not attain unto that which was their privilege. Why then was any nation ever left in darkness, from age to age, without the light of revelation to guide them? I answer, because their forefathers in some age of the world rejected revelation, cast out and killed the prophets, and turned a deaf ear to the things of God, until God took away that which they enjoyed and committed it to another people, and left them from generation to generation in ignorance, until he should see fit to send his light and truth again to that nation. But those who reject no light are under no condemnation, and the mercy of God hath claim upon them, through the blood of Christ which atoneth for the sins of the world. The heathen, who never had the light of revelation, will not be condemned for rejecting that light; while their forefathers who rejected the light are condemned; for this is their condemnation, that when light comes men reject it.

On this subject, let us examine the history of various ages: In the morn of creation men had light by direct revelation, for Adam, Cain, and Abel talked with the Lord. In the next age men had light by revelation, for Enoch walked with the Lord, and not only saw the first coming of Christ, but his second coming also, and he exclaimed:

"Behold, the Lord cometh with ten thousand of his Saints to execute judgment upon all." (y)

From which it appears that Enoch knew and prophesied concerning the Messiah, with all the plainness of an apostle. Again, in Noah's day there were positive revelations. From the days of Israel the oracles of God seemed to pertain more particularly to them, and they were chosen for that very purpose, namely, that to them might be committed the oracles of God, the priesthood, the service of God, and the promises. In process of time Israel rendered themselves unworthy of a continuance of such blessings, by stoning and killing the prophets, and by rejecting the Messiah and those that God sent unto them, until at length the Lord took the kingdom from them, as a nation, and gave it to the Gentiles, in the

(y) Jude 14, 15.

meantime winking at all the ignorance through which the Gentiles had passed. As soon as the kingdom of God was given to the Gentiles he commanded them everywhere to repent, and then if they did not do it they were under condemnation, but not before. As soon as the kingdom was taken from the Jews the fruits of it disappeared from among them, and they were dispersed among all the nations of the earth, where they have not heard the voice of inspiration, where they did not hear the voices of living prophets any more, because they rejected, persecuted, and slew those who were sent unto them in their own land. That generation of Jews who were guilty of these sins were under condemnation, and therefore they were scattered among all nations, but subsequent generations were not under this condemnation, because no prophets were sent unto them. The Savior said:

"If I had not come and spoken unto them, they had not had sin: but now they have no cloak for their sin." (z)

He also said, "This is the condemnation, that light is come into the world, and men love darkness rather than light, because their deeds are evil." (a)

When Jesus and his co-laborers brought light and truth into the world, those who rejected it were under condemnation; but, if these inspired messengers had not come, they would not have been under this condemnation, otherwise the words of the man who received only one talent would be true, when he said:

"Lord, I knew thee that thou art an hard man, reaping where thou hast not sown, and gathering where thou hast not strewed." (b)

This is not the manner of God's dealing with the children of men, for Jesus said:

"That servant which knew the Lord's will, and prepared not himself, neither did according to his will shall be beaten with many stripes. But he that knew not, and did commit things worthy of stripes, shall be beaten with few stripes. For unto whomsoever much is given, of him shall be much required: and to whom men have committed much, of him will they ask the more." (c)

Paul also said:

"The times of this ignorance God winked at, but now commandeth all men everywhere to repent." (d)

Thus we discover that the generations which have passed away without being visited by prophets or messengers from God, were not under condemnation for rejecting prophets and

(z) John 15 : 22.   (a) John 19 : 3.   (b) Matt. 25 : 24.
(c) Luke 12 47, 48.   (d) Acts 17 : 30.

messages; and, if the Spirit of God wrought upon any of them, during the dark ages which have passed away since their fathers rejected the messages which God sent unto them by Christ and his apostles, they will only be accountable for just as much light as they have received, and for no more. The Spirit of God wrought upon Columbus and by it he discovered America.

"It wrought upon other Gentiles, and they went forth out of captivity, upon the many waters." (e)

Nephi prophesied concerning the Gentiles who came to this land, and he said:

"I beheld the Spirit of the Lord, that it was upon the Gentiles, and they did prosper, and obtain the land for their inheritance. * * * * I, Nephi, beheld that the Gentiles who had gone forth out of captivity, did humble themselves before the Lord; and the power of the Lord was with them, and I beheld that their mother Gentiles were gathered together upon the land also, to battle against them; and I beheld that the power of God was upon them; and also that the wrath of God was upon all those that were gathered together against them to battle. And I, Nephi, beheld that the Gentiles that had gone out of captivity, were delivered by the power of God, out of the hands of all other nations." (f)

Thus the Spirit of God operated upon their minds by *impressions*, when they had not sufficient faith to obtain the gift of prophecy. But, in this age God has spoken from the heavens, and commissioned men to go, first to the Gentiles, commanding them everywhere to repent, and obey the gospel; and then he has commanded them to go to the Jews also, and to command them to repent and obey the gospel; thus restoring again that which has been so long lost from the earth; and, wherever their voices shall be heard, issuing this proclamation in the name of Jesus, according as He has commanded them, then and there the people are under obligation to repent and be baptized; and he that repents and is baptized shall be saved, and he that does not believe their testimony neither repent, nor is baptized, shall be damned; for this plain reason, because God has sent them, by revelation, with this message, to *this* generation; and he that rejects the least of God's ambassadors rejects him that sent him; and, therefore, they are under condemnation from that time forth; but the message which God has sent these men with is binding only on the generation to which it is sent; and is not binding at all upon those who were dead and gone before it came. Neither is it binding on any generation which shall come after, unless God

(e) Book of Mormon, 1 Nephi 3 : 36.   (f) Book of Mormon, 1 Nephi 3 : 30.

shall raise up men and send them with the same gospel; and that generation to whom he sends them will be saved or damned, according as they receive or reject the testimony of the messengers.

People frequently ask this question, saying, "If God has sent men with certain truths, which are binding on the people, and without which they cannot be saved, what will become of the good people who have died before this message came?" I answer, if they obeyed the message which God sent to their own generation, they will be saved; but if not, they will be damned. But if God sent no message to that generation, then they have rejected none, and consequently are under no condemnation, and they will rise up in judgment against this generation and condemn it; for, if they had received the same blessings which are now offered to us, they would, perhaps, have received them gladly. The principle of condemnation, in all ages of the world, is no other than rejecting the very message which God sends to that age; while they pretend to cleave closely to that which he has sent in former ages.

"Wo unto you, Scribes and Pharisees, hypocrites! because yo build the tombs of the prophets, and garnish the sepulchres of the righteous, and say, 'If we had been in the days of our fathers, we would not have been partakers with them in the blood of the prophets.' Wherefore ye are witnesses unto yourselves, that ye are the children of them which killed the prophets." (g)

This was the testimony of the Savior to the Jews, who were pretending to stand stiffly for their former prophets, and at the same time rejected Jesus and his apostles. And so it is now in the nineteenth century. You, Christians, (so-called), garnish the tombs of the Messiah and his former apostles, and even build fine chapels to their memory, entitling them St. Paul's church, St. Peter's church, St. John's church, &c.; and you say if we had lived in the days of the apostles we would not have stoned and killed them. But ye yourselves are witnesses, that ye allow the deeds of those who killed Christ and the apostles, and you build chapels in honor of them; while at the same time when a prophet or an apostle comes among you, you forthwith shut your houses against him, as soon as he testifies of what God has sent him to testify; for you say there are to be no more prophets or apostles on the earth, and forthwith pronounce him a false prophet; and if a mob rises and kills him, or burns his house, or destroys his goods, you will either rejoice, or sit in silence, and give

(g) Matt. 23 : 29-31.

countenance to the deed, and perhaps cry "false prophet," while your presses and pulpits teem with all manner of falsehoods concerning him. Wo unto you, priests, Pharisees, hypocrites; but fill ye up the measure of the ancient priests and Pharisees, for as they did, so do ye. But vengeance belongs to God, who will speedily avenge his elect, who cry unto him day and night.

But to return to the subject of revelation; "There is nothing secret that shall not be revealed; neither hid that shall not be known;" this was a maxim of the Savior. And again, "the knowledge of the Lord is to cover the earth, as the waters cover the sea." Now, I ask, how this great overturn is to be brought about? And I know no better way to answer this question, than to quote the prophecy of Nephi, in the Book of Mormon.

"For I command all men, both in the east and in the west, and in the north, and in the south, and in the islands of the sea, that they shall write the words which I speak unto them: for out of the books which shall be written I will judge the world, every man according to their works, according to that which is written. For behold, I shall speak unto the Jews, and they shall write it: and I shall also speak unto the Nephites and they shall write it; and I shall also speak unto the other tribes of the house of Israel, which I have led away, and they shall write it; and I shall also speak unto all the nations of the earth and they shall write it.

"And it shall come to pass that the Jews shall have the words of the Nephites, and the Nephites shall have the words of the Jews: and the Nephites and the Jews shall have the words of the lost tribes of Israel; and the lost tribes of Israel shall have the words of the Nephites and the Jews.

"And it shall come to pass that my people which are of the house of Israel, shall be gathered home unto the lands of their possessions; and my word also shall be gathered in one. And I will show unto them that fight against my word and against my people, who are of the house of Israel, that I am God, and that I covenanted with Abraham, that I would remember his seed forever." (*h*)

(*h*) Book of Mormon, 2 Nephi 12 : 8–10.

# AN ANALYSIS OF ISAIAH,

CHAPTER XXIX.

The first six verses of this chapter portray the degradation, distress and punishments of the inhabitants of Jerusalem, and the ruin of their city; which is completed with "the flame of devouring fire," after which "all the nations" that have been instrumental in this distress and ruin, are represented in the condition of one in a dream:

"It shall even be with them as when a hungry man dreameth, and, behold, he eateth; but he awaketh, and his soul is empty; or as when a thirsty man dreameth, and, behold, he drinketh; but he awaketh, and behold, he is faint, and his soul hath appetite; so shall the multitude of all the nations be that fight against Mount Zion."

The phrase, "the nations," usually, if not always, indicates the Gentiles; but in Luke, (a) we are told plainly that these nations are the Gentiles, who are to carry away captive the people, "and Jerusalem shall be trodden down of the Gentiles, until the times of the Gentiles be fulfilled." Hence we must look to the nations of the Gentiles for the subjects of this prophetic description of dreamy existence. The prophet says further:

"Stay yourselves, and wonder; cry ye out and cry: they are drunken, but not with wine; they stagger, but not with strong drink."

Here we find these nations of the Gentiles in a dreamy, empty, drunken, and staggering condition; and to this are added other characteristics:

"For the Lord hath poured out upon you the spirit of deep sleep, and hath closed your eyes: the prophets and your rulers, the seers hath he covered." (b)

Thus are these nations under the influence of "the spirit of deep sleep," with eyes closed, without prophets or seers.

"And the vision of all is become unto you as the words of a book that is sealed, [equivalent to saying that they shall have no vision from God], which [words] men deliver to one that is learned, saying, Read this, I pray thee: and he saith, I cannot: for it is sealed." (c)

(a) Luke 21 : 24  (b) Isaiah 29 : 10.  (c) Isaiah 29 : 11.

"And the book is delivered to him that is not learned, saying, Read this, I pray thee: and he saith, I am not learned." (*d*)

This may be called the prophetic history of what took place when the plates from which the Book of Mormon was taken came forth, as related on pages forty and forty-one of this work, which the reader is now invited to carefully examine:

"Wherefore the Lord said, Forasmuch as this people draw near me with their mouth, and with their lips do honor me, but have removed their heart far from me, and their fear toward me is taught by the precepts of men; therefore behold, I will proceed to do a marvelous work among this people, even a marvelous work and a wonder: for the wisdom of their wise men shall perish, and the understanding of their prudent men shall be hid." (*e*)

These verses show the nature of that blindness which should be prevailing when the sealed book should come forth. Drawing near to God with the mouth, and honoring him with the lips, when the heart is not in the service, marks it as a hypocritical generation. And teaching (with the lips only) the fear of the Lord by the precepts of men, shows that the religion of that day is based upon human creeds; and the marvelous work which God will do, that will destroy their wisdom and prudence, is in that he will speak as aforetime, and will re-establish his own precepts in the face of these "precepts of men," and cause the words of the sealed book to be read, which neither the wise, nor the learned and prudent could do.

That the nations of Christendom are in the condition as described above, cannot be denied. How could a state of apostasy from the gospel be better or more plainly shown? That such an apostasy would occur, and that it was foreseen by the prophets and apostles "set in the Church," is clearly shown in their writings:

"For the time will come when they will not endure sound doctrine, but after their own lusts shall they heap to themselves teachers, having itching ears, and they shall turn their ears from the truth, and be turned unto fables." (*f*)

"For I know this, that after my departing shall grievous wolves enter in among you, not sparing the flock. Also of your own selves shall men arise, speaking perverse things, to draw away disciples after them." (*g*)

"Let no man deceive you by any means, for that day, [the second coming of Christ], shall not come, except there come a falling away first, and that man of sin be revealed, the son of perdition." (*h*)

Of this anti-Christian power we are told:

"And it was given unto him to make war with the Saints, and to over-

---

(*d*) Isaiah 29 : 12.  (*e*) Isaiah 29 : 13, 14.  (*f*) 2 Tim. 4 : 3, 4.
(*g*) Acts 20 : 29, 30.  (*h*) 2 Thess. 2 : 3.

come them, and power was given him over all kindreds, and tongues and nations." (*i*)

This same power is represented under the figure of a woman upon whose forehead was her name written as follows:

"Mystery, Babylon the Great, the Mother of Harlots and Abomination of the Earth. And I saw the woman drunken with the blood of the saints, * * * with whom the kings of the earth have committed fornication, and the inhabitants of the earth have been made drunk with the wine of her fornication." (*j*)

These inhabitants of the earth "are peoples, and multitudes, and nations, and tongues." (*k*) And the same "kindreds, and tongues, and nations," are referred to in the thirteenth chapter; and these are "the multitude of all the nations" whom the prophet Isaiah saw drunken and staggering, with closed eyes and in sleep, yet drawing near to the Lord in lip service, "having a form of godliness, but denying the power thereof," "ever learning, and never able to come to the knowledge of the truth." (*l*) The cause of this situation of the nations is further manifested as follows:

"The earth also is defiled under the inhabitants thereof, because they have transgressed the laws, changed the ordinance, and broken the everlasting covenant." (*m*)

In the midst of such a condition of the nations the sealed book must come forth, and "wo unto them that seek deep [by cunning] to hide their counsel [or design] from the Lord;" for "surely your turning of things upside down shall be esteemed as the potter's clay." This clearly indicates the opposition to the marvelous work on the part of those *wise and prudent men*, among the people, who draw near to the Lord with their mouth and lips, but in their efforts to maintain the "precepts of men," against the words of the book, in their blind and drunken condition, "turn things upside down;" that is, put darkness for light, and light for darkness; calling evil good, and good evil; bitter for sweet, reversing the truth, or turning it *into a lie*. But the efforts put forth will be esteemed as crude as the potter's clay. *The remnant* of the *church* is among them, but they neither have skill nor power to reorganize the Church of Christ, any more than one unlearned in the potter's trade can form an article honorable to the art.

While this marvellous work is thus coming forth the prophet says:

(*i*) Rev. 13 : 7.  (*j*) Rev. 17 : 5, 6, 2.  (*k*) Isaiah 29 : 15.
(*l*) 2 Tim. 3 : 5-7.  (*m*) Isaiah 24 : 5.

"Is it not yet a very little while, and Lebanon shall be turned into a fruitful field, and the fruitful field shall be esteemed as a forest?" (*n*)

This fixes the date for this sealed book's coming forth, and the marvelous work accompanying it. It is a little before the sterility and barrenness of the land of Israel yields its sceptre of curse, and Lebanon becomes a fruitful field, set with its famous olive; and, so rapid will be its growth, that it will soon "be esteemed as a forest;" also, it is said, "and in that day shall the deaf hear the words of the book, and the eyes of the blind shall see out of obscurity, and out of darkness;" (*o*) and the words of the book will cause the meek also to increase their joy in the Lord, and the poor among men shall rejoice in the Holy One of Israel. (*p*) It is clear from this, that in connection with the words of the book here alluded to, the gospel is to be preached to the poor and the meek of the earth, who will receive it "gladly;" and it will increase their joy, as it did the people of Samaria at the preaching of Phillip. (*q*) And this implies a dispensation of the gospel committed from heaven at that time, as indicated by the vision of John:

"And I saw another angel fly in the midst of heaven, having the everlasting gospel to preach unto them that dwell on the earth, and to every nation, and kindred, and tongue, and people, saying with a loud voice, Fear God, and give glory to him; for the hour of his judgment is come." (*r*)

And this day or dispensation, Isaiah shows, is to be one of judgment:

"For the *terrible one* is brought to nought, and the scorner [at the marvelous work] is consumed, and all that watch for iniquity, [do iniquity in my name], shall be cut off; and that make a man an offender for a word, and turn aside the just for a thing of nought." (*s*)

Who is *the terrible one* here spoken of? Is it not that same anti-Christ-power that hath blinded and made drunk all these nations, upon whom she sits like a fatal incubus, paralyzing their moral and spiritual faculties,—priestcraft personified in the rider upon the scarlet colored beast? Hence, another voice from heaven was heard, after the gospel is restored:

"Saying, Come out of her, my people, [not my church, but the remnant of her seed], that ye be not partakers of her sins, and that ye receive not of her plagues." (*t*)

The making a man an offender for a word shows that the same pharisaical hypocrisy and self-righteous blind leaders of the blind should exist in this dispensation as in that when

(*n*) Isaiah 29 : 17.  (*o*) Isaiah 29 : 18.  (*p*) Isaiah 29 : 19.  (*q*) Acts 8 : 8.
(*r*) Rev. 14 : 6, 7.  (*s*) Isaiah 29 : 20, 21.  (*t*) Rev. 18 : 4.

Jesus came to bear testimony to the truth, when he was made an offender by this same class, of whom he said, "Except your righteousness exceed theirs, you can in *no case* enter into the kingdom of God." But, because this is an hour of judgment upon the *"terrible one,"* that has ruled the nations, who have trodden down the Holy City, and led captive her children, the promise is:

"Therefore thus saith the Lord, who redeemed Abraham, concerning the house of Jacob, Jacob *shall not* NOW be ashamed, neither shall his face NOW wax pale. They shall sanctify the Holy One of Jacob, and shall fear the God of Israel." (*u*)

What is it that shall remove the cause of Jacob's *shame* and *paleness?* Ezra says:

"O my God, I am shamed and blush to lift up my face to thee, my God; and for our iniquities have we, our kings, and our priests, been delivered into the hand of the kings of the lands, to the sword, to captivity, and to a spoil, and to confusion of face, as it is this day." (*v*)

Here it was *iniquity* and *captivity* that caused shame. So that, to remove the cause of shame in Jacob, he must return to obedience, and must be restored to his possessions. And when the before mentioned judgments are being felt, the word of promise is:

"Then look up, and lift up your heads, for your redemption draweth nigh." (*w*)

"For I would not, brethren, that ye should be ignorant, that blindness in part is happened to Israel, until the fullness of the Gentiles, [the multitude of those nations], be come in. And so all Israel shall be saved; as it is written, There shall come out of Zion the Deliverer, and shall turn away ungodliness from Jacob." (*x*)

And then Jacob need not be ashamed; for, when Jacob is saved from his captivity, he will be restored to the land of his fathers:

"Wherefore do I see every man with his hands upon his loins, as a woman in travail, and all faces are turned into paleness? * * * It is even the time of Jacob's trouble, but he shall be saved out of it. For it shall come to pass in that day, saith the Lord of hosts, that I will break his yoke [the Gentiles] from off thy neck; therefore fear thou not, O my servant Jacob, saith the Lord; neither be dismayed, O Israel; for lo, I will save thee from afar, and thy seed from the land of their captivity; * * * for I am with thee, saith the Lord, to save thee; though I make a full end of all nations whither I have scattered thee. * * * I will bring again into the captivity of Jacob's tents, and have mercy on his dwelling-places." (*y*)

"Behold, I will take the children of Israel from among the heathen,

(*u*) Isaiah 29 : 22, 23.   (*v*) Ezra 9 : 6, 7.   (*w*) Luke 21 : 28.
(*x*) Romans 11 : 25, 26.   (*y*) Jer. 30 : 6–18.

whither they be gone, and will gather them on every side, and bring them into their own land; and I will make them one nation upon the mountains of Israel; and one king shall be king to them all: and they shall be no more two nations, neither shall they be divided into two kingdoms any more at all." (z)

This restoration is still in the future, and when the *times* of this *restitution* come, it is the fullness of the times of the Gentiles, and the time of deliverance for Jacob; hence this is the reason why he "shall not now be *ashamed*, neither shall his face *now* wax pale."

Another characteristic of the time of the coming forth of the sealed book, and of the marvelous work, is indicated as follows!

"They also that erred in spirit shall come to understanding, and they that murmured shall learn doctrine." (a)

Spirit phenomena has, in the present age, developed more diversity of opinion, and consequently more error, than any age preceding. And, such is the uncertainty and anxiety of the public mind, that some stable criterion, by which to judge, is pressingly demanded; and here is promise that in this time shall be developed the means by which those *erring* in *spirit* shall come to *understanding*. This has been done already, in part, by the restoration of the spiritual gifts promised to the believer; among which "discerning of spirits" is received, and visions of the spirit state vouchsafed, enabling those who are exercised therein to trace spirit manifestation to their proper source.

"And they that *murmured* shall *learn doctrine.*" Creedology, the creature of the apostasy, born in the dark ages, when "ignorance was the mother of devotion," and arrogance the framer of articles of faith and intolerance, does not sit lightly upon the soul and conscience of the nineteenth century. The better part of those who know what they are, though nurtured up in their profession, do not believe them, but *murmur* in their hearts against them. These shall, in the day of the *marvelous work*, and the coming forth of the sealed book, *learn doctrine*, the true doctrine of Christ, when they shall cease to murmur, and joy and rejoicing take its place.

In order to confirm our interpretation and application of the twenty-first and twenty-second verses of Isaiah twenty-ninth chapter, that they refer to the near approach of Israel's restoration to their own land, we cite the fact that, though it has been, since their dispersion, a barren waste, and a thirsty

(z) Ezek. 37 : 21, 22. (a) Isaiah 29 : 24.

land, yet that it is now, even as in former times, blessed with the former and the latter rain, and with copious dews of heaven developing its former fertility, and that they are actually now returning, rebuilding, and enjoying the renewed fatness of their land, thus being prepared for them according to promise.

We annex the following testimony:

"An important society has been formed in Europe, called The International Society of the Orient, to prevent the grave complications arising out of the Eastern Question and to regenerate the East, by infusing therein the spirit of Western civilization. To accomplish this great result, the Society, which enrolls among its members, such men as Napoleon, Rothchilds, and Montefiore, proposes to favor the development of agriculture, industry, commerce, and public works in the East, especially in Palestine; to obtain from the Turkish government certain privileges and monopolies, chief of which is the gradual concession and advancement of the lands of Palestine; to distribute at cash prices such of those lands as the company receives, and to effect the colonization of the most fertile villages of the Holy Land. The Society, after having established its commercial bureau at Constantinople and other cities of the Turkish empire, will construct a port at Joppa, and a good road, or railroad, from that city to Jerusalem. Upon the north of this road, the Society expects land to be ceded by Turkey, which they will sell to Israelitish families. These, in their turn, will create new colonies, aided by their Oriental co-religionists, and it is expected special committees will send thither Jews of Morocco, Poland, Moldavia, Wallachia, from the East, and from Africa. The Society claim that the plan will reconstruct the holy places of Jerusalem in a Christian manner, put an end to the constant conflict between the great powers in reference to them, transform the ancient Jerusalem into a new and great city, create European colonies, which will become, in time, the centers, whence Occidental civilization will spread in Turkey and penetrate to the remote Orient. The Society is being rapidly formed, with the strongest influences, financial and political at its back. The Rothchilds, Mores, Montefiore, and other great capitalists among the Jews, are actively in sympathy with the undertaking. The plan has also the favor of more than one crowned head in Europe, amongst them, Napoleon, of whose special theories of nationalities it is a development. Several prominent noblemen of England, and the leading names of the Faubourg St. Germain are also among its friends." (*b*)

"It [Palestine] has the same bright sun and unclouded sky, as well as the *early* and *latter rain*, which, however, is diminished in quantity, owing to the destruction of trees." (*c*)

The following is from a recent traveler in that country:

"I arrived in Indiana a few days since, from the Eastern Continent. I stopped at Joppa nearly the whole winter. For my part I was well pleased with the country. It is certainly a land of most wonderful

(*b*) Chicago Tribune, Oct. 2, 1866.   (*c*) Chambers' Encyclopedia, vol 7, p. 11.—Palestine.

fruitfulness, with a delightsome climate, producing everything, if properly cultivated, and from two to three crops in a year. They have grain, fruit and vegetables all the year round; in fact I never was in such a country before. I have seen much good country in Europe and America, but none to compare with Palestine; its fruitfulness is uncommon, and the climate the most delightsome; even in winter I did not see the least sort of frost, and vegetables of every sort were growing in perfection in gardens. It is a *fact* that *the rain and dew* are *restored;* recently, in 1853, *the former and the latter rain were restored,* to the *astonishment of the natives.* The Jews have been returning to the Holy Land for some time, and are increasing, going to their beloved Canaan from many parts of Europe, Asia and Africa. They are making preparations to rebuild cities and [build] railroads. The fruit in Palestine is better than in Europe and America. They have camels, mules, horses, asses, cattle, sheep and goats; but I saw no hogs. The natives are generally friendly." (*d*)

"The result of Dr. Barclay's observations is to show that the greatest fall of rain at Jerusalem in a single year was eighty-five inches, and the smallest forty-four, the mean being 51 1-6. These figures will be best appreciated by recollecting that the average rain fall at London during the whole year is only twenty-five inches, and that in the wettest parts of the country, such as Cumberland and Devon, it rarely exceeds fifty inches. As in the time of our Savior, (Luke 12: 54), the rains come chiefly from the south, or south-west; they commence at the end of October, or beginning of November, and continue with greater or lesser constancy till the end of February, or middle of March, and, occasionally, though rarely, till the end of April. Between April and November, there is, with the rarest exception, an uninterrupted period of fine weather, and skies without a cloud. During the summer the dews are very heavy, and often saturate the traveler's tent, as if a shower had passed over it. The nights, especially towards sunrise, are very cold, and thick fog or mists are common all over the country. Thunder storms of great violence, are frequent during the winter months." (*e*)

Surely, from these testimonies, Jerusalem can no more be called a thirsty land, nor a barren waste, (*f*); but rather Lebanon has indeed become "a fruitful field."

J. W. BRIGGS.

(*d*) Louis Van Buren, Sen., Nov. 14, A.D. 1867.  (*e*) Dic. of Bible, by Wm. Smith, page 636.—Art. Palestine.  (*f*) Ezek. 5:14; 38:8.

# THE DOCTRINE OF CHRIST

—— AND THE ——

## FALSE DOCTRINES OF THE NINETEENTH CENTURY

CONTRASTED.

"Whosoever transgresseth, and abideth not in the doctrine of Christ, hath not God. He that abideth in the doctrine of Christ, he hath both the Father and the Son."—2 John 9v.

### DOCTRINE OF CHRIST *versus* DOCTRINES OF MEN.

D. OF C.—"These signs shall follow them that believe." Mark 16:17.

D. OF M.—These signs shall not follow them that believe, for they are done away, and no longer needed.

D. OF C.—"In my name shall they cast out devils." 17v.

D. OF M.—In His name they shall not cast out devils.

D. OF C.—"They shall speak with new tongues." 17v.

D. OF M.—The gift of tongues is no longer needed.

D. OF C.—"They shall take up serpents, and if they drink any deadly thing, it shall not hurt them. They shall lay hands on the sick, and they shall recover." 18v.

D. OF M.—If they take up serpents they will bite them. If they drink any deadly thing, it will kill them. They shall not lay hands on the sick and they recover; for these things are done away.

D. OF C.—"He that believeth on me, the works that I do shall he do also, and greater works than these shall he do, because I go to the Father." John 14:12.

D. OF M.—He that believeth on Christ, shall not do any of the miracles and mighty works that He did, for such things have ceased.

D. OF C.—"There is nothing secret that shall not be revealed, neither hid that shall not be known." Luke 8:17.

D. OF M.—There is to be no more revelation, for all things necessary are already revealed.

D. OF C.—"He shall send His angels, and they shall gather His elect from the four winds," &c. Mat. 24:31.

D. OF M.—There is to be no more ministering of angels, for such things are done away.

D. OF C.—"I saw an angel flying in the midst of heaven, having the everlasting gospel to preach to them that dwell on the earth." Rev. 14: 6.

D. OF M.—Angels do not appear in this enlightened age, because they are no longer needed.

D. OF C.—"When he, the Spirit of truth is come, he will guide you into all truth, * * * and he will shew you things to come." John 16: 13.

D. OF M.—Inspiration is no longer needed in this age of learning and refinement. The Spirit will not show you things to come, for then you would be a prophet, and there are to be no prophets in these days.

D. OF C.—"If ye abide in me, and my words abide in you, ye shall ask what ye will, and it shall be done unto you." John 15: 17. "If ye shall ask any thing in my name I will do it." John 14: 14.

D. OF M.—It is not so in these days. We must not expect to heal the sick and work miracles, consequently we must not expect to receive what we ask for.

D. OF C.—"Neither pray I for these alone; but for them also which shall believe on me through their word: that they all may be one; as thou, Father, art in me, and I in thee, that they also may be one in us: that the world may believe that thou hast sent me." John 17: 20, 21.

D. OF M.—We are all good Christians, and we all believe on Him through the apostles' words, although we are divided into several hundred different sects.

D. OF C.—"One Lord, one faith, one baptism." Eph. 4: 5.

D. OF M.—Many lords, many faiths, and three or four kinds of baptism.

D. OF C.—"By one Spirit are ye all baptized into one body." 1 Cor. 12: 13.

D. OF M.—By many spirits are we all torn asunder into different bodies.

D. OF C.—"He (Christ) gave some apostles, and some prophets, and some evangelists, and some pastors, and some teachers, for the perfecting of the Saints, for the work of the ministry, for the edifying of the body of Christ." Eph. 4: 11.

D. OF M.—There are to be no more apostles, and no more prophets. But the work of the ministry, the perfecting of the Saints, and the edifying of the *different* bodies of Christ, can all be done very well without these gifts of God; only give us money enough to educate and employ the wisdom of men.

D. OF C.—These gifts and offices were to continue "till we all come in the unity of the faith, and of the knowledge of the Son of God, unto a perfect man, unto the measure of the stature of the fulness of Christ." 13v.

D. OF M.—Apostles, miracles, and gifts, were to continue during the first age of christianity, and then they were to cease, because no longer needed, having accomplished their purpose.

D. OF C.—These gifts and offices were given "that we henceforth be

D. OF M.—Tracts, creeds, sermons and commentaries of uninno more children, tossed to and fro, and carried about with every wind of doctrine, by the sleight of men, and cunning craftiness, whereby they lie in wait to deceive." 14v.

D. OF C.—"No man taketh this honor unto himself, but he that is called of God, as was Aaron." Heb. v. 4.

D. OF C.—"How shall they preach except they be sent?" (of God). Rom. 10: 14.

D. OF C.—"Is any sick among you? Let him call for the elders of the Church; and let them pray over him, anointing him with oil in the name of the Lord: and the prayer of faith shall save the sick, and the Lord shall raise him up; and if he have committed sins, they shall be forgiven him." Jas. 5: 14, 15.

D. OF C.—"Repent, and be baptized every one of you in the name of Jesus Christ, for the remission of sins, and ye shall receive the gift of the Holy Ghost. For the promise is unto you, and to your children, and to all that are afar off, even as many as the Lord our God shall call." Acts 2: 38, 39.

D. OF C.—"It shall come to pass in the last days, saith God, I will pour out of my Spirit upon all flesh: and your sons and your daughters shall prophesy, and your young men shall see visions, and your old men shall dream dreams." 17v.

D. OF C.—"Follow after charity, and desire spiritual gifts, but rather that ye may prophesy." 1 Cor. 14: 1.

D. OF C.—"Covet to prophesy, and forbid not to speak with tongues." 38v.

D. OF C.—"In vain they do worship me, teaching for doctrines the

spired men, together with a hireling priesthood, are now necessary in order to keep men from being carried about with every wind of doctrine, &c.

D. OF M.—No man taketh this honor unto himself but he who has been educated for the purpose, and commissioned by men.

D. OF M.—How shall they preach except they be well educated for the purpose, and sent by the board of officers.

D. OF M.—If any are sick among you do not send for the elders of the Church; or if the elders come, do not let them lay hands on them, neither let them anoint them in the name of the Lord, for this is all a Mormon delusion, but send for a good physician, and perhaps you may get well.

D. OF M.—Repent and come to the anxious seat, or mourners' bench, every one of you, and cry "Lord, Lord," and you will get forgiveness of sins; but you may be baptized or not; but if you are baptized, you will not get the Holy Ghost as they did anciently, for such things are done away.

D. OF M.—In these last days the Lord will *not* pour out of His Spirit, so as to cause our sons and daughters to prophesy, our old men to dream dreams, and our young men to see visions; for such things are no longer needed, and it is a delusion, and none but the ignorant believe such things.

D. OF M.—Do not covet any of the supernatural gifts, but especially beware of prophesying, for such things are done away.

D. OF M.—Do not prophesy, and it is entirely a delusion to speak in tongues.

D. OF M.—It matters not what kind of doctrine, or what system a commandments of men." Mat. 15:9.

D. OF C.—"I thank thee, O Father, Lord of heaven and earth, because thou hast hid these things from the wise and prudent, and hast revealed them unto babes. Even so, Father, for so it seemed good in thy sight." Mat. 11: 25, 26.

D. OF C.—"No man knoweth the Son but the Father, neither knoweth any man the Father save the Son, and he to whomsoever the Son will reveal him." 27v.

D. OF C.—"This is life eternal, that they might know Thee, the only true God, and Jesus Christ whom thou hast sent." John 17: 3.

D. OF C.—"I thank my God always on your behalf, for the grace of God which is given you by Jesus Christ, that in every thing ye are enriched by him in all utterance, and in all knowledge, even as the testimony of Christ (the Spirit of prophecy) was confirmed in you, so that ye come behind in no gift, waiting for the coming of our Lord Jesus Christ." 1 Cor. 1: 4–7.

D. OF C.—"The foolishness of God is wiser than men, and the weakness of God is stronger than men. For ye see your calling brethren, how that not many wise men after the flesh, not many mighty, not many noble are called: but God hath chosen the foolish things of the world, to confound the wise, and God hath chosen the weak things of the world, to confound the things which are mighty; and base things of the world, and things which are despised, hath God chosen; yea, and things which

man embraces, if he is only sincere, and worships Jesus Christ.

D. OF M.—We thank God that he has revealed nothing to any person, wise or simple, for many hundred years, but that our wise and learned men have been able to know God without revelation, and that we shall never be favored with any more.

D. OF M.—We all know God in this enlightened age, and yet neither the Father nor the Son has revealed any thing to any of us, for we do not believe revelations are necessary now.

D. OF M.—We cannot know for ourselves, by any positive manifestation in these days, but must depend on the wisdom and learning of men.

D. OF M.—We thank the Lord always in behalf of the church in these days, that she has no supernatural gifts given unto her, and that she is not enriched by Christ, neither in the gift of utterance, nor in the gift of knowledge, neither has she the testimony of Jesus (the Spirit of prophecy) confirmed in her, and she comes behind in all the gifts; nor is she waiting for, nor expecting the coming of the Lord, for he has come once, and never will come again till the great and last day, the end of the earth.

D. OF M.—The wisdom of men, and the learning of men is better than the inspiration of the Almighty, for that is not needed any longer; for you see your calling brethren, how that the wise and learned, and noble and the mighty, are called in these days, for we have chosen such to confound the foolish, the unlearned, and the ignorant; yea, to confound the base things of the world which are despised, that flesh might glory in his presence.

are not, to bring to nought things that are; that no flesh should glory in his presence." 1 Cor. 1: 26-29.

D. OF C.—"I, brethren, when I came to you, came not with excellency of speech; or of wisdom, declaring unto you the testimony of God; for I determined not to know any thing among you, save Jesus Christ, and him crucified; and I was with you in weakness, and in fear, and in much trembling; and my speech and my preaching was not with enticing words of man's wisdom; but in demonstration of the Spirit, and of power; that your faith should not stand in the wisdom of men, but in the power of God." 1 Cor. 2: 1-5.

D. OF C.—"But we speak the wisdom of God in a mystery, even the hidden wisdom, which God ordained before the world unto our glory; which none of the princes of this world knew, for had they known it, they would not have crucified the Lord of glory." 7, 8v.

D. OF C.—"But God hath revealed them unto us by his Spirit; for the Spirit searcheth all things, yea the deep things of God." 10v.

D. OF C.—"For what man knoweth the things of man, save the spirit of man which is in him? Even so the things of God knoweth no man but the Spirit of God." 11v.

D. OF C.—"Now we have received not the spirit of the world, but the Spirit which is of God; that we might know the things that are freely given to us of God." 12v.

D. OF C.—"Which things also we speak, not in the words which man's wisdom teacheth, but which the Holy Ghost teacheth, compar-

D. OF M.—We, brethren, when we came unto you, came with excellency of speech, and with the wisdom and learning of man, and our speech, and our preaching were with enticing words of man's wisdom, not in demonstration of the Spirit, and power, for this is done away; that your faith should not stand in the power of God, but in the wisdom of man.

D. OF M.—We speak the wisdom of men, in a mystery, even the hidden wisdom which none but the learned know, for had others known it, they would never have been under the necessity of employing us to tell it to them.

D. OF M.—But God hath revealed nothing unto us by His Spirit; for the wisdom and learning of men searcheth all things; yea, all the deep things which are necessary for us to know.

D. OF M.—For what man knoweth the things of man, save the spirit of man which is in him; even so the things of God knoweth no man by the Spirit of God, in these days; for it is done away, and it reveals nothing.

D. OF M.—Now we have not received the Spirit of God, but the spirit of the world, that we might not know for a certainty, but that we might guess at, or give our opinion, of the things of God.

D. OF M.—Which things also we speak not in the words which the Holy Ghost teacheth, but which man's wisdom teacheth, for the ing spiritual things with spiritual." 13v.

D. OF C.—"But the natural man receiveth not the things of the Spirit of God, for they are foolishness unto him; neither can he know them, because they are spiritually discerned." 14v.

D. OF C.—"Let no man deceive himself. If any man among you seemeth to be wise in this world, let him become a fool, that he may be wise." 1 Cor. 3:18.

D. OF C.—"For the wisdom of this world is foolishness with God, for it is written, 'He taketh the wise in their own craftiness;' and again, 'the Lord knoweth, the thoughts of the wise, that they are vain.' Therefore let no man glory in men." 19–21v.

D. OF C.—"Now concerning spiritual gifts, brethren, I would not have you ignorant." 1 Cor. 12:1.

D. OF C.—"For the manifestation of the Spirit, is given to every man to profit withal." 7v.

D. OF C.—"For to one is given by the Spirit the word of wisdom; to another the word of knowledge by the same Spirit." 8v.

D. OF C.—"To another, faith by the same Spirit; and to another, the gift of healing by the same Spirit." 9v.

D. OF C.—To another, the working of miracles, to another, prophecy; to another, discerning of spirits; to another, divers kinds of tongues; to another, the interpretation of tongues." 10v.

D. OF C.—"For as the body is one, and hath many members, and all the members of that one body being many, are one body, so also is Christ." 12v.

inspiration of the Holy Ghost is done away.

D. OF M.—But the learned man may receive and understand the things of God, by his own wisdom, without the inspiration of the Spirit, for who will be so foolish as to believe in visions and revelations in this religious age.

D. OF M.—Let no man deceive himself. If any man among you seems to be wise in the things of God, let him get the wisdom of men, that he may be wise.

D. OF M.—For the wisdom of God is foolishness with the world; for it is written, let us educate young men for the ministry, and let no man preach who has not been educated for the purpose, and we will receive no man who professes to be inspired.

D. OF M.—Now concerning spiritual gifts, brethren, we would have you entirely ignorant, for they are not needed at all in this generation.

D. OF M.—For the manifestation of the Spirit is given to no man to profit at all.

D. OF M.—But to one is given by the learning of men, the word of wisdom; and to another the word of knowledge by human learning.

D. OF M.—God gives to another faith, by the same Spirit, but to none the gift of healing by the same Spirit.

D. OF M.—God gives to none the working of miracles, and to none to prophesy, and to none discerning of spirits, and to none to speak with divers kinds of tongues, and to none to interpret tongues.

D. OF M.—For as the body is composed of many sects and parties who are opposed to each other, and have no gifts, and being many sects, are but one body, so also is Christ.

D. OF C.—"For by one Spirit are we all baptized into one body, whether we be Jews or Gentiles; whether we be bond or free, and have been all made to drink into one Spirit." 13v.

D. OF M.—By many spirits we are all baptized into many bodies, whether we be Catholics or Protestants, Presbyterians or Methodists, but have all drank into one spirit, even the spirit of the world.

D. OF C.—"For the body is not one member, but many." 14v.

D. OF M.—The body is not one sect, but many.

D OF C. "But now hath God set the members every one of them in the body, as it hath pleased him." 18v.

D. OF M.—Now hath the God of this world set the sects and parties [in the body of Antichrist] as it hath pleased him.

D. OF C.—"And if they were all one member, where were the body?" 19v.

D. OF M.—If they were all one sect, where were the body?

D. OF C.—"But now are they many members, yet one body." 20v.

D. OF M.—Now are they many sects, yet but one body [even Babylon.]

D. OF C.—"Now ye are the body of Christ, and members in particular." 27v.

D. OF M. Now ye are the bodies of Christ, [Antichrist] and members in particular.

D. OF C.—"And God hath set some in the Church, first, apostles; secondarily, prophets; thirdly, teachers; after that miracles, then gifts of healings, helps, governments, diversities of tongues." 28v.

D. OF M.—Man hath set some in the Church; first a hired minister; second a board of officers; thirdly, tracts; then commentaries, creeds, diversities of opinions, societies, and wondrous helps.

D. OF C.—"Blessed are ye when men shall revile you, and persecute you, and shall say all manner of evil against you falsely, for my sake. Rejoice and be exceedingly glad, for great is your reward in heaven; for so persecuted they the prophets which were before you." Matt. 5: 11, 12.

D. OF M.—Woe unto you when men revile you, and persecute you, and say all manner of evil against you falsely, for Christ's sake. Lament ye, and be exceedingly sorrowful in that hour, for little is your reward among men, for so they do to the Latter Day Saints.

D. OF C.—"Give to him that asketh thee, and from him that would borrow of thee, turn thou not away." 42v.

D. OF M.—Give to him that asketh of thee, if he be able to make thee a similar present ; and from him that would borrow of thee, turn thou not away if he be able to pay thee again with interest.

D. OF C.—"Be ye therefore perfect; even as your Father who is in heaven is perfect." 48v.

D. OF M.—Do not think to be perfect; for it is impossible to live without sin.

D. OF C.—"Take heed that you do not your alms before men, to be seen of them, otherwise you have

D. OF M.—Take heed that you do your alms before men, to be seen of them; otherwise you have

D. OF C.—"Therefore when thou doest thine alms, do not sound a trumpet before thee as the hypocrites do, in the synagogues, and in the streets, that they may have glory of men. Verily I say unto you, they shall have their reward." 2v.

D. OF M.—When thou doest thine alms, publish it in the *Missionary Herald*, or some other paper, that you may get praise of the world. Verily I say unto you, you shall have your reward.

D. OF C.—"And when thou prayest, thou shalt not be as the hypocrites are, for they love to pray standing in the synagogues, and in the corners of the streets, that they may be seen of men." 5v.

D. OF M.—When thou prayest, be like the hypocrites in days of old; go before the public and cry mightily, not expecting to be heard and answered, for that would be miraculous, and miracles have ceased.

D. OF C.—"Moreover when ye fast, be not as the hypocrites, of a sad countenance, for they disfigure their faces, that they may appear unto men to fast. Verily I say unto you, they have their reward." 16v.

D. OF M.—Moreover when ye fast, be like the hypocrites, of a sad countenance, that they may appear unto men to fast; so that you may get your reward.

D. OF C.—"Lay not up for yourselves treasures upon earth, where moth and rust doth corrupt, and where thieves break through and steal, but lay up for yourselves treasures in heaven, where neither moth nor rust doth corrupt, and where thieves do not break through and steal, for where your treasure is, there will your heart be also." 19-21v.

D. OF M.—Lay up for yourselves abundance of treasures on the earth, where moth and rust doth corrupt, and where thieves break through and steal, for if your heart is only in heaven, it is no matter how rich you are in this world; for now it is come to pass that ye can serve God and Mammon.

D. OF C.—"Therefore all things whatsoever ye would that men should do to you, do ye even so to them; for this is the law and the prophets." Mat. 7:12.

D. OF M.—Therefore all things whatsoever men do to you, do ye even so to them, for this is the law and the *practice*.

D. OF C.—"Enter ye in at the strait gate, for wide is the gate and broad is the way, that leadeth to destruction, and many there be which go in thereat." 13v.

D. OF M.—Enter ye in at the wide gate where the multitude go, for it cannot be that all our great and learned men are wrong, and nobody right but a few obscure individuals.

D. OF C.—"Because, strait is the gate, and narrow is the way that leadeth unto life, and few there be that find it." 14v.

D. OF M.—For the narrow way is not only altogether too strait, but only a very few travel in it.

D. OF C.—"Beware of false prophets, which come to you in sheep's clothing, but inwardly they are ravening wolves. Ye shall know them by their fruits. Do men gather grapes of thorns or figs of thistles?" 15, 16v.

D. OF M.—Beware of prophets who come to you with the word of God, you may know at once they are false without hearing them or examining their fruits; for popular opinion is against them; whereas if they were men of God, the people would speak well of them.

D. OF C.—"By their fruits ye shall know them. Not every one that saith unto me Lord, Lord, shall enter into the kingdom of heaven, but he that doth the will of my Father who is in heaven." 20, 21v.

D. OF M.—If we are only sure that we have experienced religion, and if we pray often, we shall be saved, whether we do the Lord's will or not; for it mattereth not what system we embrace, whether it is right or wrong, if we are only sincere.

D. OF C.—"And it came to pass when Jesus had ended these sayings, the people were astonished at his doctrine, for he taught them as one having authority, and not as the scribes." 28, 29v.

D. OF M.—And it came to pass when men had ended all these sayings, the people were pleased with their doctrines, for they taught them not as one having authority, but as the scribes.

---

### RETURNING TO ZION.

Daughter of Zion, from the dust,
  Exalt thy fallen head;
Again in thy Redeemer trust,
  He calls thee from the dead.

Awake, awake, put on thy strength,
  Thy beautiful array;
The day of freedom dawns at length—
  The Lord's appointed day.

Rebuild thy walls, thy bounds enlarge,
  And send thy heralds forth,
Say to the south, "Give up thy charge,"
  And "Keep not back, O north."

They come! they come! thine exiled bands;
  Where'er they rest or roam,
They've heard thy voice in distant lands,
  And hasten to their home.

Thus, though the present world shall burn,
  And God his works destroy,
With songs His ransom'd shall return,
  With everlasting joy.

---

Printed at the Herald Office, Plano, Kendall Co., Illinois.

www.ingramcontent.com/pod-product-compliance
Lightning Source LLC
Chambersburg PA
CBHW020115170426
43199CB00009B/533